WOOD JOINTS

By Machine & By Hand

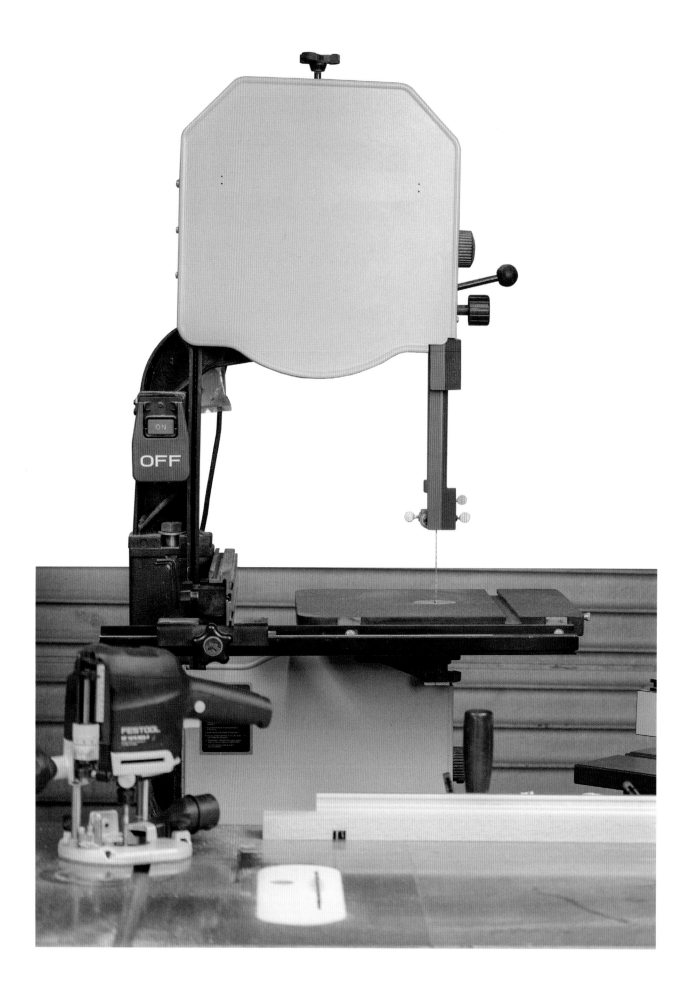

WOOD JOINTS
By Machine & By Hand

Randall A. Maxey

WOOD JOINTS BY MACHINE AND BY HAND

CONTENTS

WOODWORKING JOINTS

Woodworking is an inherently dangerous pursuit. Readers should not attempt the procedures described herein without seeking training and information on the safe use of tools and machines, and all readers should observe current safety legislation in your country.

Where applicable, guards have been removed for photographic clarity and in some places fingers are pointing at a process without the machine running.

WOOD JOINTS BY MACHINE AND BY HAND

Woodworking is a craft that generally splits folks into two groups. One group prefers the speed and convenience of machinery like tablesaws and routers to get the job done. They enjoy the process of getting the most out of their shop equipment and relish the opportunities to use them for their projects.

Others prefer the slower pace and a more peaceful atmosphere that using hand tools provides. For them, there's something about working with a more hands-on approach. Measuring, marking, cutting, hand planing, and chiseling at the workbench provides a quieter method to creating joinery. Not to mention the skills that develop and the satisfaction you get without the excess noise and sawdust machines produce.

Of course, there are benefits to both styles of woodworking and there is certainly no right or wrong way to complete the joinery. For speed and efficiency in cutting multiple, repeatable joints as in a production run of several identical pieces, machines certainly excel. But there are times when using hand tools takes less time than it would to set up a machine.

In this book, we present a variety of common woodworking joints and how to make them. We show you at least two methods to create each joint. Using hand tools for joinery, you'll develop and improve your skills with hand saws, chisels, and hand planes. For those that lean toward the power tool side, we also demonstrate how you can make the same joint with tools like tablesaws, bandsaws, and routers. As you work your way through this book, you may find yourself becoming a "hybrid" woodworker—using a combination of hand tools and machinery. As a matter of fact, if you create a joint with power tools, you may find yourself using hand tools for the final fitting. The result is a gap-free, strong joint, regardless of the methods and tools used.

One lesson that both new and seasoned woodworkers should remember is that getting great results requires practice. As you gain experience laying out joinery, using your tools, and assembling the joint, you'll find that your skills get better over time.

So, sharpen those chisels and dust off the power tools. As you work your way through each of the joints in this book, take your time. Slow down. Take deep breaths. Relax. Learn how to use your tools more effectively. You'll soon be creating joinery and projects that you'll be proud to show off to friends and family.

Stay sharp,

Randy

DADO JOINT

Commonly used to provide strength for shelves in bookcases, the dado joint has many other uses, as well. It provides a solid mechanical connection and plenty of glue surface for a solid joint.

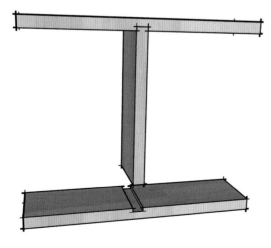

The joint is made by forming a dado, or groove, in one piece, for example, the side of a bookcase, to fit the end of the adjacent piece such as a shelf.

BY HAND

TOOLS NEEDED:

- Saw
- Chisels
- Hand plane
- Shoulder plane
- Router plane
- Combination square
- Clamps

Conventional woodworking nomenclature dictates that a "groove" runs parallel to the grain of the wood while a "dado" runs across, or perpendicular to, the grain.

1 Locate the dado on the workpiece and scribe a line that defines one shoulder of the dado.

2 Using a workpiece the same thickness as the adjoining piece, lay out the opposite shoulder of the dado, using a square to accurately position the second workpiece.

3 Transfer the shoulder lines to the edges of the workpiece to the desired depth of the dado.

4 A marking gauge is a great tool to lay out the dado depth. Set the proper depth using a steel rule.

5 Use the marking gauge to scribe the lines defining the bottom of the dado. Be sure to reference the same face of the workpiece when marking each edge.

6 The scribed line defining the bottom of the dado should intersect the shoulder lines.

7 It's always a good idea to mark the waste area to be removed.

8 Using the widest chisel available, set the cutting edge into the scribed shoulder line with the bevel of the chisel facing the waste. A couple of firm taps helps define a clean edge for the dado's shoulder. Work across the shoulder line on both sides of the dado.

9 Repeat the process of defining the shoulder edges using a chisel. Note that the bevel of the chisel is still facing the waste area.

10 With the bevel of the chisel facing down, position the cutting edge within the waste area about 1/16in to 1/8in away from the shoulder line.

11 Make a few firm taps on the chisel with a mallet to remove a thin slice of material, stopping at the shoulder line. This notch serves as a guide, often called a knife wall, for the hand saw when cutting the dado.

12 Position the blade of the saw within the notch you formed with a chisel, making sure the teeth of the saw are tight against the shoulder line. Cut down both shoulders to the marked depth of the dado.

13 If needed, use a guide block to help keep the saw blade square to the face of the workpiece as you saw the shoulders of the dado.

14 Using a chisel approximately as wide as the dado, remove the waste by taking thin slices, working deeper with each pass.

15 Keep removing waste with the chisel until the depth almost reaches the marked depth of the dado.

16 Use the chisel to pare away any remaining material, using the marked depth as a guide. Again, keep the bevel of the chisel facing the waste area.

17 To create a smooth dado bottom, a shoulder plane is ideal. The blade of the plane extends out to the edges to allow planing into a corner.

18 Another option for smoothing the bottom of a dado and fine-tuning the depth is to use a router plane. The L-shaped blade adjusts in fine increments to sneak up on the final depth.

19 Test the fit of the second, adjoining piece into the dado. Make any fine adjustments with a sharp chisel until the joint closes tight with no gaps.

WORKSHOP NOTES

COMBINATION/PLOW PLANE
A combination or plow plane, with its wide assortment of blades, is capable of cutting dadoes and grooves in a range of common widths. Shown here is an antique combination plane (bottom) with a modern plow plane (top).

BY MACHINE

A tablesaw makes cutting dadoes and grooves easy. For those tablesaws that accept a dado blade, it's a matter of setting the blade width and making the cut. To make dadoes and grooves with a single blade, make a number of passes as shown here.

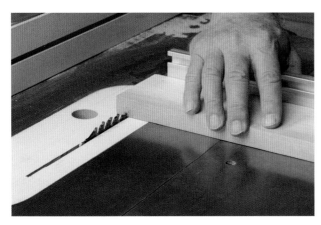

1 Set the height of the saw blade to equal the desired depth of the dado. Using a miter gauge to position the workpiece, align one shoulder line of the dado marked on the edge of the workpiece with the edge of the tablesaw blade, keeping the blade in the waste area.

2 Make a pass to define one shoulder of the dado.

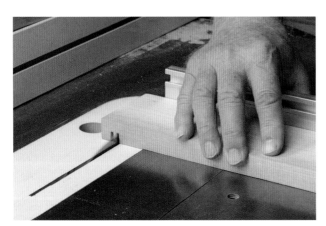

3 Realign the workpiece to cut the opposite shoulder and make another pass.

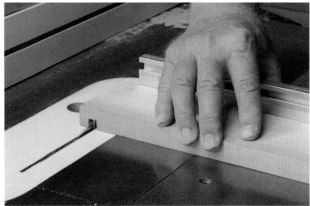

4 Make minor adjustments to the position of the workpiece to remove the remaining waste in multiple passes over the blade.

TIP

A router table presents another option for cutting dadoes using a straight bit. See the Lap Joints on pages 42–49, which are similar to extra-wide dadoes.

5 A final pass over the blade should result in a dado with a flat bottom and crisp shoulder lines.

The dado joint used in shelving.

EDGE JOINT

Use the edge joint when gluing up wide panels from narrow boards. Common uses for this joint include tabletops and cabinet doors. If you don't have access to stock wide enough for the job, glue up narrow stock to create a wide panel. The edges of a board are defined by the surfaces adjacent to the wider faces. An edge joint gains its strength from the large surface area for glue along the long-grain edge.

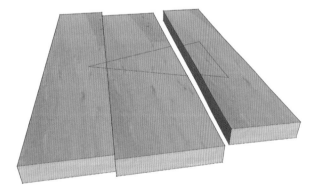

To construct a strong edge joint, prepare the stock by planing it to thickness and jointing each edge. Cut the boards to length and rough width as determined by the final size of the panel, leaving a little extra to trim after the panel is glued up.

Take time to arrange the boards to minimize the appearance of glue lines and for a pleasing appearance across the panel. To make it easier to glue the boards in their proper location and orientation, mark a "carpenter's triangle" across the entire panel. Then you can address and glue up each joint, aligning the pencil lines of the triangle.

BY HAND

As a rule, I like to use a jointer plane on the edges of the stock to be glued. The 22in to 24in (550mm to 610mm) length of a jointer plane rides over the high spots, cutting them down as you plane until the edge is smooth and straight.

1 The long body of a jointer plane makes it ideal for creating a smooth glue surface. Joint one edge before marking the piece for its final width.

2 Referencing off the jointed edge of the workpiece, use a marking gauge or combination square to indicate the final width of the workpiece.

3 Use a rip saw to cut the piece to width, making sure to cut on the waste side of the marked line.

4 Use a hand plane to remove saw marks, planing down to the marked line.

5 Arrange the boards for the best appearance and mark a triangle across all the pieces. This aids in orienting each piece during glue-up.

6 For each pair of boards, rotate each piece with the glue edge facing up. Clamp the pair in the bench vise with the top edges flush and plane until the edges are smooth. Planing the pair of boards together eliminates any error in the planing angle, resulting in a gap-free joint.

7 When planing each pair of boards for an edge joint, if the plane isn't perfectly square (shown exaggerated), it will not matter. The angle on each board complements the other in the assembled joint.

8 When the planed edges are assembled, the complementary angles create a perfect, gap-free joint.

9 Apply a thin layer of wood glue to the edges.

10 Apply clamps with just enough pressure to draw the joint tight.

BY MACHINE

Using power tools to create an edge joint follows roughly the same process as using hand tools. Instead of using a hand saw to rip pieces to width, use the tablesaw. And if you don't have access to a hand plane to remove saw marks, use a sanding block to smooth the edges for glue-up, being careful not to round over the edges.

One tablesaw accessory you may want to purchase is a rip blade designed to leave a smooth edge. Conventional rip blades are designed to hog away material in the most efficient manner but leave a rough edge. Glue-line rip blades, however, are specially made with a tooth configuration that leaves an edge suitable for glue-up without any sanding or planing.

Lacking a glue-line rip blade, a jointer comes in handy for creating smooth, straight edges for joinery.

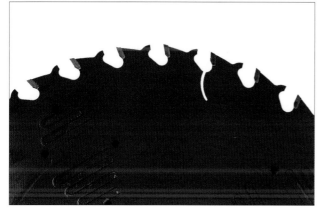

1 A glue-line rip blade is manufactured to provide a smooth edge, ready for glue-up, when ripping boards to width.

2 Use a jointer to smooth the edges and faces of each workpiece in preparation for joinery.

BUTT JOINT

End-grain butt joints are useful in building boxes or frames for cabinets and doors. A butt joint is created by fastening the end grain of one piece to the face or edge grain of the adjacent piece.

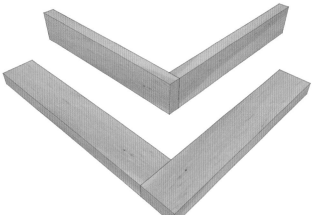

A butt joint is the easiest joint to make however, it has the reputation of being one of the weakest joints. Traditionally, wood glue didn't hold its strength when applied to end grain. The glue would wick into the grain leaving little on the surface. Many woodworkers reinforce the joint with nails, screws, or other fasteners.

BY HAND

TOOLS NEEDED:

- Saw
- Hand plane
- Shooting board

With the reputation for weak butt joints when using glue, it's easy to underestimate the strength of modern wood glues. Properly applied, wood glue forms a very strong joint for most applications. If the joint is going to encounter a lot of stress, it's best to also reinforce the joint with additional hardware.

1 Start by cutting the workpieces to length. Here, I'm using a bench hook to aid in making a square cut.

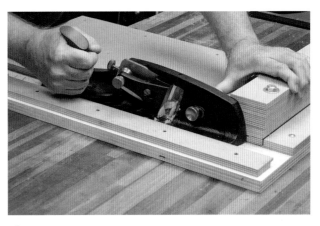

2 Use a shooting board to make sure the end grain of each workpiece is smooth and square for glue-up.

3 With all the workpieces cut to length, it's time for glue-up. One thing to remember is that end grain will soak up some of the glue. I like to apply a layer of glue to the end grain, wait a couple of minutes, then apply another thin layer before assembly.

4 Once you have applied a couple of thin layers of glue to the end grain, assemble and clamp the joint.

WORKSHOP NOTES

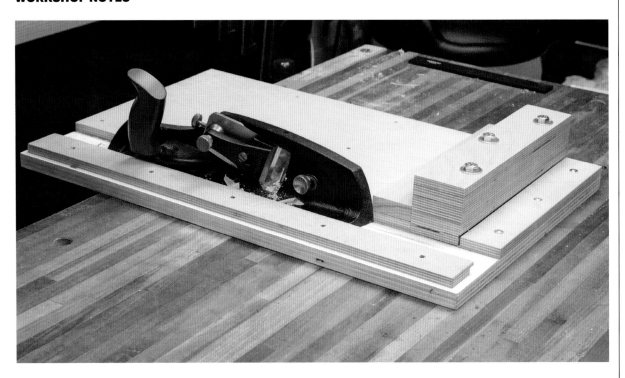

SHOOTING BOARD AND SHOOTING PLANE

A shooting board (sometimes called a "chute" board) excels at squaring up the ends and edges of a workpiece. The fence holds the workpiece square to a track designed to guide a hand plane. A specialty miter plane, shown here, features a sole with the bed and side at 90° and a skewed blade to make a slicing cut across end grain. Shooting boards also work great to square up the long edges of a workpiece.

You can make a simple shooting board using a bench hook and turning your hand plane on its side to ride across the benchtop with the sole against the edge of the bench hook. The key to any shooting board is a fence that's square to the edge the plane follows to make the cut.

BY MACHINE

TOOLS NEEDED:

- Tablesaw or miter saw

Making butt joints or end joints by machine only requires a tablesaw or miter saw. The quality of the blade determines the final quality of the joint.

1 Whether you use a miter saw or tablesaw, use a saw blade specifically designed for cutting across the grain to cut the workpieces to length. The large number of teeth ensure a smooth cut ready for glue-up.

2 Once the workpieces are cut to length, test to make sure the joint is square by dry-fitting the pieces. Gluing and assembling the joint goes quick. Just remember to apply a couple of thin layers of glue to the end grain before clamping.

RABBET (REBATE) JOINT

Rabbet (rebate) joints are particularly useful for drawer and box construction. Each joint is made up of a shoulder and cheek formed at right angles to one another to create a step, or notch, in the workpiece. The added glue surface provided by the rabbeted piece contributes to the joint's strength.

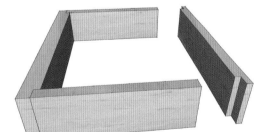

Left: Rabbet joints create strong assemblies for boxes and drawers.

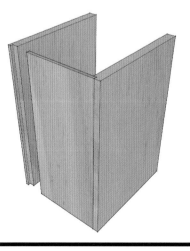

Right: Rabbet joints cut along the back edges of cabinet sides create ideal joinery for cabinet backs.

BY HAND

TOOLS NEEDED:
• Saw
• Chisels
• Hand plane
• Shoulder plane
• Router plane

When cutting rabbet joints by hand, hand saws and sharp chisels make cutting a rabbet joint on the end of a workpiece (cross-grain), like a drawer front, an easy task.

Hand-cut rabbet joints with the grain along the edge of a workpiece benefit from specialized rabbeting planes designed for such tasks.

1 Define the shoulder and depth of the rabbet using a marking gauge to scribe guidelines for cutting the rabbet.

2 Create a knife wall at the shoulder by removing small, shallow chips from the waste side up to the scribed line. Use the chisel with the bevel down to provide a pivot point for controlling the depth of cut.

3 Cut the shoulder of the rabbet using a crosscut saw, cutting down to the scribed cheek (depth) line.

4 Use a rip saw to cut the cheek down to the shoulder kerf, staying on the waste side of the scribed line. You can use a crosscut saw, if necessary, but it will take a bit longer to complete the cut.

5 Clean up the cheek and shoulder using a router plane or shoulder plane, working down to the scribed lines.

WORKSHOP NOTES

RABBET PLANE

A hand plane designed to cut rabbets features a cutting iron (blade) that extends to the sides of the plane, enabling it to make shavings the full width of the plane. Two other features make rabbet planes easy to use. A movable fence positions the cutting edge of the plane to define the width of the rabbet.

The key is to apply pressure to the fence, keeping it in contact with the face of the workpiece. The depth stop, as the name suggests, determines the final depth of the rabbet. When the stop contacts the workpiece, the plane stops cutting.

A specialized rabbet plane, such as this Stanley No. 78 Duplex Rabbet Plane, makes quick work of cutting rabbets by hand.

This modern Veritas Skew Rabbet plane features an angled cutting edge suitable for making smooth cuts.

BY MACHINE

TOOLS NEEDED:
• Tablesaw (or router table with a straight bit or a rabbeting bit)

There are several options available for using power tools to create rabbet joints. Your choice depends on the tools and accessories you have available.

Here, we present three methods:

A. Using a tablesaw to make two cuts that define a rabbet.
B. Using a straight bit in a table-mounted router.
C. Using a rabbeting bit in a router table.

A. CUTTING A RABBET WITH A TABLESAW

The tablesaw is an effective tool for cutting rabbets. You can do so with two cuts: one to define the depth of the rabbet and another to define the width. You can also make multiple passes over the saw blade to remove waste. Whichever method you use, it all starts with accurate layout (refer to Photo 1 on page 25).

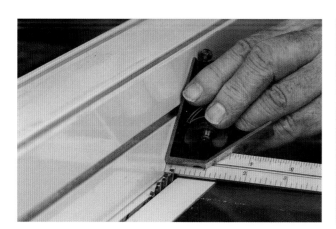

1 Set the tablesaw rip fence as a stop to define width of rabbet. Make sure the saw blade is on the waste side of the line with the stock against the fence. Set the height of the blade to just touch the layout line for the depth of the rabbet.

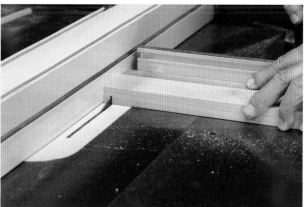

2 For cuts across the grain, use a crosscut or combination blade to cut the shoulder of the rabbet, double-checking depth of cut. A backer board helps eliminate chipping and tearout as the blade exits the workpiece.

3 There are two methods you can use to remove the waste. Without moving the rip fence, make multiple passes over the blade.

4 With a tall auxiliary fence attached to the tablesaw fence or a tall sled to support the workpiece, cut so the waste falls away from the blade without getting trapped between the blade and fence.

B. CUTTING A RABBET USING A STRAIGHT BIT AT THE ROUTER TABLE

Using a straight bit at the router table provides a quick and easy way to create rabbets. With a straight bit, the maximum width of the rabbet is dependent upon the diameter of the bit. It is common practice to use a bit with a diameter larger than the desired rabbet width. This allows for fine adjustment simply by repositioning the fence on the router table.

You have a choice when it comes to selecting a straight bit. Conventional straight bits feature two or three cutting edges that run parallel to the axis of the bit. This style of bit is inexpensive but is not the ideal choice for heavy use and where the quality of the cut matters.

Solid-carbide spiral router bits, while being more expensive, leave a smooth surface and excel at removing chips without risk of burning. When shopping for a spiral bit, you see terms like "upcut" and "downcut." These simply refer to the direction of the spiral on the bit and how the chips are ejected. A downcut spiral bit leaves a smooth surface on the face of the workpiece, especially on plywood. An upcut spiral bit excels at removing chips but at a slightly higher risk of chipout on the face of the workpiece.

1 When using a straight bit to form a rabbet, the router table fence sets the width of the rabbet. It's a good idea to sneak up on the final depth of the rabbet by making light passes, raising the bit slightly between passes.

C. USING A RABBETING BIT AT THE ROUTER TABLE

Rabbeting bits are typically large-diameter bits with a bearing that rides against the workpiece and determines the width of the rabbet. Rabbeting bits are available for cutting rabbets of a predefined width. This is dictated by the diameter of the bearing included with the bit. Another, more flexible option, is to purchase a rabbeting bit set which includes bearings in a range of diameters for cutting rabbets in a variety of widths with one router bit.

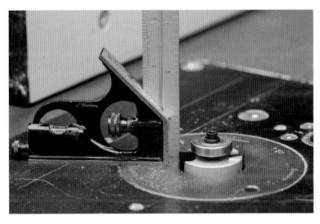

1 Set the height of the rabbet bit using a combination square. For smoother cuts, make a shallow pass then raise the bit slightly between passes until you reach the final depth of the rabbet.

2 After installing a rabbet bit, set the fence flush with the bearing using a straightedge as a guide. The fence helps support the workpiece on straight cuts, yielding a smoother cut.

3 When cutting a rabbet on the end of a workpiece at the router table, use a backer board to help guide the workpiece.

TONGUE-AND-DADO JOINT

Capitalizing on a mechanical, interlocking joint, the tongue-and-dado is often used to construct solid drawers and boxes. It features a dado on one piece that fits onto a tongue on the adjacent piece. In this case, a tongue is formed by creating a rabbet.

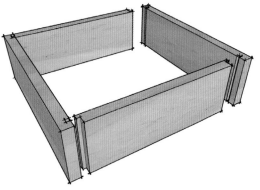

Left: For drawers, the sides feature dadoes. The tongue at each end of the front and back parts of the drawer fits into its corresponding dado. This method of construction ensures the drawer front remains solid with repeated opening and closing of the drawer.

BY HAND

TOOLS NEEDED:
- Marking gauge
- Marking knife
- Combination square
- Saw
- Chisels
- Hand plane
- Shoulder plane
- Router plane

When laying out a tongue-and-dado joint, locate one shoulder of the dado based on the thickness of the adjoining piece. The width of the dado is a matter of personal choice, but a good rule of thumb is half the thickness of the adjoining piece. On ¾in (19mm) thick workpieces, for example, locate one shoulder of the dado ¾in (19mm) from the end of the workpiece. Lay out the other shoulder 3/8in (10mm) from the end of the workpiece.

For the depth of the dado, it's a good idea to make it half the thickness of the workpiece or less. Any deeper would compromise the strength of the joint.

CUTTING A DADO

1 Use a square and the adjoining workpiece to locate one shoulder of the dado.

2 Without moving the square, define the shoulder line with a marking knife.

3 Set the depth of the marking gauge to locate the opposite shoulder of the dado.

4 Mark the second shoulder line that defines the width of the dado.

5 It's helpful to mark the waste areas to avoid cutting on the wrong side of the line.

6 To prepare for marking the tongue on the adjoining piece, use the same depth of the marking gauge you used to define the second shoulder of the dado.

7 Using the outside face of the workpiece as a reference, mark a line across the end using the marking gauge to define the thickness of the tongue that will fit in the dado.

8 Continue the lines around to the edges of the workpiece.

9 With the marking gauge set to the desired depth of the dado, mark the width of the rabbet that forms the tongue. Take this opportunity to also mark the depth on the edges of the dado workpiece.

10 After marking the edges of the workpiece to define the length of the tongue, the notch (rabbet) should be evident.

11 Mark the waste areas to clarify what material needs to be removed to create the tongue-and-dado joint.

12 To double check your markings, assemble the workpieces as they would be oriented in the finished joint.

13 Set the cutting edge of a wide chisel in the scored line with the bevel facing the waste area. Make a few firm taps with a mallet to more clearly define the shoulders of the joint.

14 With the bevel of the chisel facing down, place the cutting edge about 1/16in to 1/8in (1.5mm to 3mm) away from the scored lines. A few firm taps with a mallet removes a sliver of material to form a notch that guides the saw later.

15 With the blade of a hand saw tight against the shoulder line and in the notch, cut down to the depth of the dado. A block of wood can assist in keeping the saw blade square to the workpiece as you cut.

16 After sawing to define the dado width, use a chisel to remove the waste. Remove a small amount at a time, gradually working down to the marked depth of the dado.

17 As you approach the marked depth, begin paring away material, using the depth line as a guide.

18 To ensure square shoulders on joinery, it's helpful to use a guide block clamped to the workpiece at the marked shoulder line to keep the chisel square to the workpiece as you pare away the waste.

CREATING THE TONGUE

19 On the adjoining workpiece that fits into the dado, use the same saw techniques you used when cutting the dado to cut the shoulder line of the rabbet that forms the tongue.

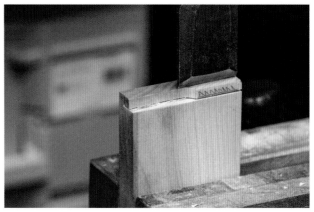

20 Use a chisel to gradually remove the waste, keeping the bevel facing the waste.

21 As you approach the marked thickness of the tongue, carefully pare away the waste to the line.

22 Clean up any remaining, excess material with a sharp chisel.

23 A small shoulder plan makes cleaning up and fine-tuning the fit of the joint an easy task.

24 Check the fit of the joint and make any adjustments necessary until the joint fits snugly without gaps. If the joint is too tight, don't force it to as you could damage one of the parts.

I like to cut the dadoes first then fine-tune the fit of the tongue in the dado. Forming the tongue is simply a matter of cutting a rabbet on the opposite face of the tongue. Locate the shoulder of the rabbet a distance from the end of the workpiece equal to the width of the dado

WORKSHOP NOTES

SMALL SHOULDER PLANE

A small shoulder plane is a great tool for cleaning up narrow rabbets to form tongues. Small joinery planes like this are handy for fine-tuning the fit of joints.

BY MACHINE

TOOLS NEEDED:
- Marking gauge
- Marking knife
- Combination square
- Tablesaw
- Shoulder plane
- Chisel

The tablesaw is a great tool for cutting the dado and tongue. The router table with a straight bit makes another great option. Here, we focus on using the tablesaw.

The layout work for marking the dado and tongue is the same as that shown before for making the joint with hand tools.

CUTTING A DADO

1 Set the height of the saw blade to match the depth of the dado. Align the blade on the waste side of the line marking the dado shoulder.

2 Make the cut to create one shoulder of the dado.

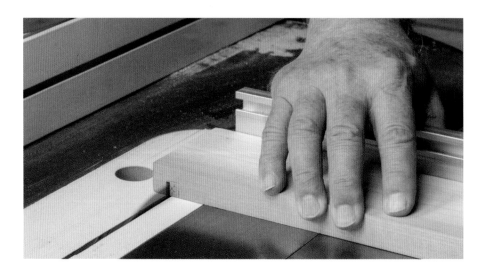

3 Repeat the process to cut the other shoulder, keeping the blade to the waste side of the line.

4 Make several passes over the blade, moving the workpiece slightly to carefully remove all the material between the shoulders.

CUTTING A DADO

5 With the saw blade height set to the depth of the rabbet that creates the tongue, make a pass to define the shoulder, keeping the blade to the waste side of the line.

6 Make a pass at the end of the workpiece to create a clean edge for the tongue.

7 Make a few passes over the blade to remove the remaining waste, slightly adjusting the position of the workpiece between each pass.

8 Check the fit of the joint and note any tight areas.

9 In spite of using a power tool to cut the joint, a hand tool such as a shoulder plane is the best tool to fine-tune the thickness of the tongue to fit the dado. A chisel is also a good option to pare away any high spots.

10 Keep checking your progress by test-fitting the joint until it fits snugly with no gaps.

LAP JOINT

Lap joints are appropriate for a variety of cabinet face frame and door frame constructions. Opposing notches in the pieces overlap and form a solid connection. Plenty of glue surface makes the joint very strong. Variations of the lap joint include an end-lap, T-lap, and cross-lap.

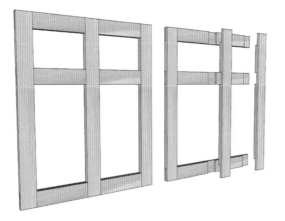

One goal to keep in mind when making lap joints is to make the faces of the intersecting workpieces flush with one another. It's best to work with workpieces the same thickness to make layout and cutting the joints easier.

BY HAND

Making a lap joint with hand tools starts with careful layout and marking. Then, after making straight cuts with a saw and carefully removing the waste with a chisel, you're well on your way to a tight-fitting joint.

CROSS AND TEE LAP JOINTS

1 Determine the location for the lap joint and scribe a line that defines one edge of the joint.

2 The adjoining workpiece dictates the location of the opposite edge of the notch. Place the knife in the first scribed line, butt the workpiece against the knife blade, then use a square to temporarily orient the second workpiece. Holding the square tight, remove the workpiece and scribe along the blade of the square to define the second edge of the notch.

3 With the knife edge on the scribed line at the corner of the workpiece, butt a saddle square against the knife and scribe a line on the edge of the workpiece to the midpoint.

4 To define the baseline, or bottom, of the notches use a marking gauge to scribe a line between the two previously scribed edges of the notch.

5 Place the edge of a chisel in the scribed line with the bevel facing the waste to be removed. The wider the chisel, the smoother your cut lines will be. Firmly tap the chisel with a mallet to define the edges of the joint. Repeat the process across the workpiece and the opposite scribed line.

6 With the workpiece secure on the benchtop, place the chisel bevel-down about 1/8in (3mm) from the chiseled line. Make sure the chisel is resting on the waste material to be removed. Make a couple of light taps to form a small V-notch. Stop at the scribed line and remove the chips. This V-notch forms a registration point for the saw.

7 An easy way to remove the waste is to make several parallel saw cuts down to the baseline of the joint.

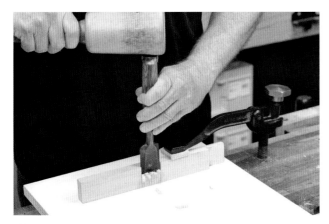

8 Use a wide chisel to remove the waste. The saw cuts make it an easy task to pop the chips free.

9 A router plane features a narrow blade that extends below the base of the plane. A knob adjusts the height of the blade. A router plane is a great tool for applications like this where you need to ensure a flat surface at the bottom of the joint.

10 Use a wide chisel to shave off any remaining waste. Use the baseline as your guide. A sharp chisel is a must to get good results.

11 A shoulder plane makes a great addition to your toolbox. It allows you to clean up joinery for a perfect fit.

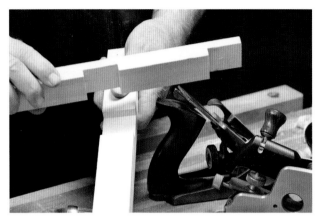

12 Test the fit of the joint frequently to sneak up on a perfect, gap-free joint where the faces of the two workpieces are flush with one another.

13 The satisfaction of a perfect fit makes all that work worthwhile.

END LAP JOINT

1 Rest the teeth of the saw in the V-notch. Saw down to the baseline.

2 For T-lap or end-lap joints, clamp the workpiece vertically and cut along the waste side of the baseline to remove the waste.

3 There are many methods you can use to clean up and smooth the bottom of the notches. A wide chisel is one way to get the job done. Work down to the scribed baseline.

4 A shoulder plane is another handy tool for cleaning up and fine-tuning the fit of lap joints. The plane's blade is flush with the sides of the plane, making it ideal for fitting into corners.

5 Use a shoulder plane on its side to clean up the shoulder of the notch.

6 These specialized rabbet planes feature a skewed cutting blade that extends flush with one side of the plane. They're available in right-hand and left-hand versions. These are also great tools for tweaking the fit of joinery.

7 Make fine cuts with a skewed rabbet plane to finesse the fit of lap joints.

WORKSHOP NOTES

SHOULDER PLANES

Shoulder planes were designed for a specific task: removing saw marks and cleaning up the shoulders of tenons and lap joints. The blade of a shoulder plane is flush with the sides, making it ideal for getting into corners.

But shoulder planes are much more versatile than this specialized task. They are one of the best tools for fine-tuning the fit of a variety of joints including dadoes, rabbets, tenons, and grooves.

Shoulder planes are available in a wide range of sizes and shapes. Purchasing a shoulder plane is one of the best investments you can make as a woodworker.

BY MACHINE

TOOLS NEEDED:

• Tablesaw

Everything mentioned previously regarding laying out lap joints applies when you use power tools like a tablesaw to make the joint.

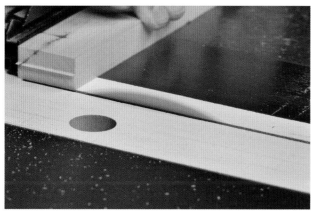

1 To set the blade height on the tablesaw, use a scrap piece the same thickness as the workpieces used for making the joint. Make a narrow cut across the end of the workpiece. Flip the workpiece over and repeat the cut. Adjust the blade height until the blade just removes the remaining waste.

2 Using a miter gauge, align the workpiece so the blade cuts to the inside of the shoulder lines. Make both cuts to define the two shoulders of the notch.

3 Make repetitive cuts between the two shoulders to remove the bulk of the waste.

4 Once the majority of the waste is removed, test the fit of the joint. Make any adjustments using the tools and techniques shown in the previous section.

MORTISE-AND-TENON JOINT

A mortise and tenon joint earned its reputation over the millennia as a very strong joint used in carpentry and furniture construction. You'll find it used in cabinet face frames, paneled doors, and table bases, to name just a few examples.

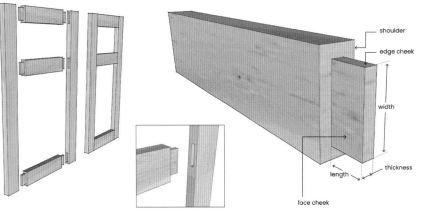

A tenon, or tongue, formed on the end of one piece fits into a mortise (slot) on the adjacent piece. The mechanical connection provides plenty of glue surface to create a time-tested, strong joint.

BY HAND

TOOLS NEEDED:
- Saddle square
- Marking gauge
- Chisels
- Saws

It's a debate among woodworkers whether you should make the mortise first or the tenon. If you choose to make the mortises first, it's easier to fine-tune the fit of the tenon for a strong joint. However, if you choose to make the tenon first, you can use it to lay out the mortise size. My preference is to make the mortise first and fit the tenon later. Here, I lay out the mortise and the tenon at the same time but cut the mortises first.

MORTISE

1 A mortise is an open slot that accepts a tenon. There are a variety of methods you can use to cut mortises.

2 If you have multiple parts requiring mortises, gang them together as shown to keep the mortise location consistent. Lay out the location and size of mortise on the workpiece. Use a square to keep the ends of the mortise square to the face of the workpiece.

3 A marking gauge creates precise, incised lines that mark the sides (cheeks) of the mortise. When sizing the width of the mortise to be cut with chisels, use the width of the chisel as a guide.

TIP

When using a marking gauge to lay out the mortises and tenons, marking from each face of the workpiece without changing the gauge distance will automatically center the mortise on the width of the workpiece.

4 Use a chisel closest in width to the width of the mortise. Place the chisel on the end of the mortise with the bevel facing the waste (mortise). A couple of firm taps with a mallet define the ends of the mortise.

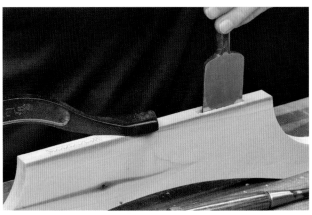

5 Use a wide chisel to deepen the scored lines defining the length of the mortise. Use caution here. Tapping too hard can split the wood along the grain.

6 A mortise chisel features a thick, strong blade designed for chopping and prying waste out of the mortise. You can also use a standard bench chisel but use care when prying to avoid breaking the blade. Tap firmly along the mortise, creating smaller chips to remove.

7 Use the chisel to remove the chips. You don't need to go too deep. You'll work in stages, gradually working to the full depth of the mortise.

8 After removing the chips, repeat the process of defining the ends and walls of the mortise, then prying out the chips as above. Clean out the bottom of the mortise to create a flat bottom.

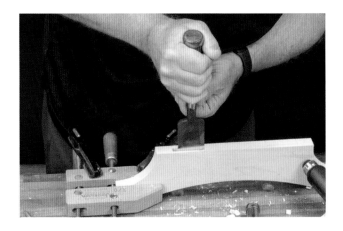

TENON

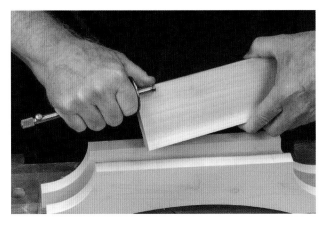

9 Now you'll lay out and cut the tenon to fit the mortise. Most of your layout work here is best accomplished with a marking gauge. It scores clean, straight lines that serve as guidelines for your chisel or saw.

Mark the length of the tenon on all four sides of the workpiece using a marking gauge. These lines define the shoulders of the tenon.

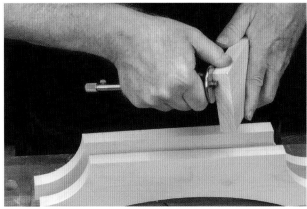

10 Reset the marking gauge to define the thickness of the tenon, using the mortise width as a guide.

> **TIP**
>
> **Marking the mortise width and tenon thickness at the same time with the same setting on the marking gauge creates a more accurate joint.**

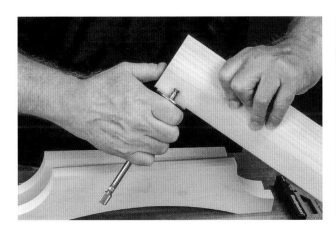

11 Mark the edge cheeks by starting at one shoulder line, scribing to the end of the workpiece, wrapping around the end, then across the opposite face, stopping at the shoulder line on the opposite face.

12 Use a pencil to trace over the scribed lines, making them easier to see when it comes time to form the tenon.

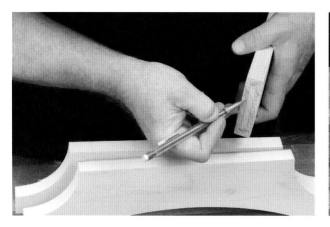

13 Marking the waste area before making cuts is always a good idea.

14 To form a groove or "knife wall" for the hand saw, start by defining the shoulders of the tenon with a few firm taps of the chisel placed in the scored layout line.

15 Position the cutting edge about 1/16in (1.5mm) to 1/8in (3mm) to the waste side of the shoulder line. Make a couple of light taps to remove a narrow chip, creating a shallow groove.

16 Place the blade of the hand saw in the groove, tight against the shoulder line. Saw down to the line defining the thickness of the tenon.

TIP

Cutting the shoulders of the tenon first provides definitive stopping points for the saw when cutting the cheeks of the tenon.

17 Use the same process to cut the side cheeks, cutting down to the line defining the width of the tenon.

18 Orient the workpiece vertically to saw the side cheeks down to the shoulder.

19 Use the marking gauge to redefine the thickness of the tenon.

20 Using the edge and end layout lines as guides, saw the face cheeks down to the shoulder line.

21 Check the fit of the tenon in the matching mortise. It's best to have the tenon too tight rather than too loose. This way, you can sneak up on the fit using planes and chisels.

22 Pare away excess material using a sharp chisel, cutting down to the layout lines.

23 A shoulder plane helps clean up the shoulders of the tenon.

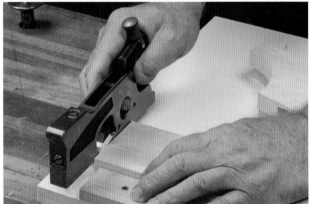

24 The shoulder plane also makes an ideal tool for removing thin shavings until the tenon fits the mortise. Work from both sides to keep the tenon centered.

25 Before assembly, chamfering the edges at the end of the tenon makes it easier to assemble and allows some space for excess glue.

26 Make one final test of the fit of the tenon, making any necessary adjustments until it fits snug. If the tenon is too loose, it creates a weak joint.

WORKSHOP NOTES

SKEW BLOCK PLANE

This is a truly versatile plane. It excels at trimming rabbets, working end grain, or making final jointing cuts on boards, plus you can use it in all the ways you would a regular block plane.

The blade is skewed at a 15° angle, which makes cutting easier, either with or across the grain, and helps pull the fence tight against the work. Because the blade sits flush with the side of the body, corner cuts are clean and accurate.

BY MACHINE

There are numerous ways to cut a mortise to accept a tenon. A router table and drill press are good options. A mortising machine (mortiser) is specially built for cutting mortises.

A. DRILL PRESS

1 A bradpoint drill bit drills clean holes without skipping or wandering off the target center point.

2 Drill each end of the mortise, staying just inside the layout lines. Drill holes between to remove the bulk of the waste. You'll still have to do a little handwork to clean up the walls of the mortise with sharp chisels.

B. ROUTER TABLE

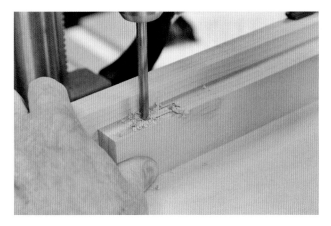

1 Before routing a mortise at the router table, drill a start and stop hole at each end of the mortise.

2 The holes you drilled slip over a straight router bit in the router table.

A spiral upcut bit (center) cuts clean mortises with less burning than traditional straight bits.

TIP

While you can use any straight bit in the router table to cut mortises, you'll get better results using a carbide spiral bit. While more expensive than traditional straight bits, spiral bits are designed to cut quickly and cleanly. For routing mortises, look for an upcut spiral bit. It removes chips from the mortise efficiently, keeping the bit cooler.

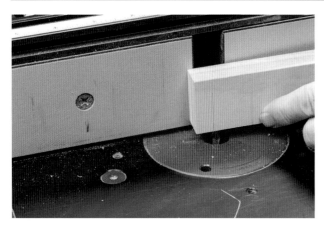

3 When routing mortises at the router table, make several passes, raising the bit between each pass, until you reach the final mortise depth.

4 Layout lines on the front of the workpiece serve as a guide when routing the length of the mortise. You'll feel when the router bit reaches the predrilled hole at the end of the mortise.

5 After routing the mortise, you can either square up the ends of the mortise with a chisel or round over the corners of the tenon prior to assembly.

C. MORTISING MACHINE (MORTISER)

WORKSHOP NOTES

MORTISER

A mortising machine (right) is similar to, but a much more stoutly built, drill press. It features a movable fence to position the workpiece under the bit and a hold-down to prevent uplift when drilling mortises. The long handle provides leverage for lowering the bit for cutting mortises.

Left: A mortising machine features a specialized bit for drilling square holes. The drill bit fits inside a hollow, square chisel.

Right: The square chisel on the mortising bit forms a square hole in the workpiece while the internal drill bit removes the waste and ejects it through the opening in the chisel body.

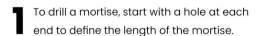

1 To drill a mortise, start with a hole at each end to define the length of the mortise.

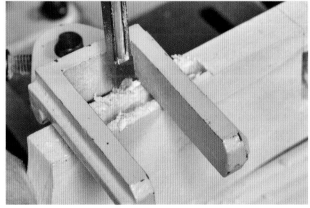

2 Drill out the waste by making several overlapping passes, moving the workpiece after each pass. Clean up the mortise walls with a sharp chisel.

BRIDLE JOINT

The tenon and mortise of the bridle joint are just variations of the mortise-and-tenon joints shown on pages 50–61 and the methods to cut them are very similar.

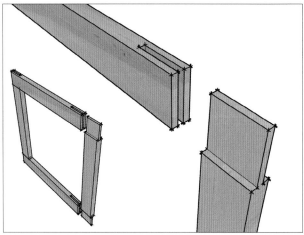

Above: A bridle joint is handy for building doors and cabinet frames.

Left: One piece, with a tongue (tenon) formed on the end, fits into a mating slot (mortise) on the adjacent piece.

BY HAND

TOOLS NEEDED:

- Precision square
- Marking gauge
- Chisels
- Hand saw
- Coping saw
- Shoulder plane
- Mortise chisel
  or bench chisel
- Skew block plane

The interlocking nature of the bridle joint provides plenty of mechanical strength and glue surface for a strong joint. As with most joints, the key is in the preparation with accurate measuring and marking.

1 Set the marking gauge to the width of the workpiece. Extending the gauge another fraction of an inch leaves the assembled joint a little proud to plane or sand flush after assembly.

2 Use the marking gauge at this setting to mark the shoulders of the tenon and depth of the notch, or mortise.

3 Reset the marking gauge to mark the cheeks of the tenon and mortise. A good rule of thumb is one-third the thickness of the workpiece.

4 Mark the edges and ends of each workpiece to lay out the thickness of the tenon and width of the mortise.

5 Mark the waste area to be removed. This serves as a visual reminder on which side of the line to cut to create the joint.

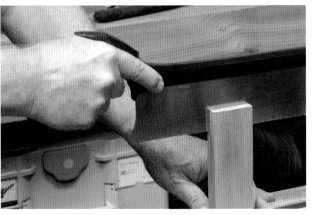

6 Saw on the waste side of the line to cut both cheeks of the mortise. Use the layout lines on the edges and end of the workpiece to help guide the saw.

7 As with the mortise, saw on the waste side of the layout lines down to the shoulder line to create the tenon.

8 Use a wide chisel to deepen the shoulder line with a few firm taps on the chisel.

9 With the bevel of the chisel facing down, remove a thin chip along the shoulder line to create a clean, definitive starting line for the saw.

10 Use a saw to cut down to the shoulder line to complete the tenon.

11 After test-fitting the joint, use a shoulder plane to remove saw marks and gradually sneak up on a snug fit.

12 Another great option for tweaking the fit of the tenon is using a wide chisel to pare away material.

13 A coping saw is the perfect tool for removing the remainder of the waste left from cutting the mortise cheeks. Leave a small amount of material at the bottom of the mortise to clean up with a chisel.

14 Use a mortise chisel or bench chisel to clean up the bottom of the mortise. The width of the chisel should match the width of the mortise.

15 Clean up the inside walls of the mortise with a sharp chisel.

BY MACHINE

TOOLS NEEDED:

- Precision square
- Marking gauge
- Tablesaw
- Toggle clamps

The layout for marking the bridle joint to machine is the same as that shown for making the joint with hand tools. A tablesaw is a great power tool for cutting these joints. The trick is that the workpieces must be oriented vertically and securely for clean cuts.

1 This shop-made jig fits over the rip fence and includes a pair of toggle clamps to secure the workpiece. Be mindful of the blade height and make some test cuts.

2 To cut the cheeks of the tenon, align the blade on the waste side of the line. The blade height matches the length of the tenon.

3 Make one pass over the blade to define one cheek.

4 Rotate the workpiece 180° without moving the jig and make another pass. This automatically centers the tenon on the thickness of the workpiece.

5 Lower the blade to make the shoulder cuts without cutting into the tenon. Use a stop block clamped to the rip fence ahead of the blade to position the workpiece. The stop block prevents the workpiece from binding on the blade and causing kickback.

6 Use the miter gauge to position the end of the workpiece against the stop block and guide the workpiece across the blade to cut one shoulder. Flip the workpiece over and repeat for the other side.

7 Use the tenon workpiece to position the jig for cutting the mortise. Align the outside of the blade with the outside of the tenon cheek.

8 Make a pass over the blade to cut one cheek of the mortise.

9 Rotate the workpiece 180° and repeat the cut. There will likely be some remaining waste to be removed.

10 Reposition the jig to remove the waste from the mortise.

11 Check the fit of the bridle joint. The joint should be snug with no gaps. After assembly, sand or plane the joint smooth.

12 A bandsaw makes quick work out of cutting the mortise and tenon of a bridle joint. Position the workpiece using a fence to keep the blade on the waste side of the layout lines.

DRAWBORED (PEGGED) MORTISE-AND-TENON JOINT

Making the drawbored joint is identical to a standard mortise and tenon joint (see pages 50–61) with the addition of pegs or dowels. Whether you create the mortise and tenon with hand tools or power tools, the process of creating a drawbore joint is identical for both.

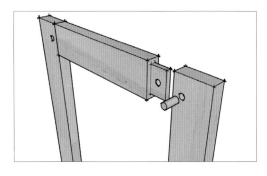

The size and number of pegs you use is a matter of personal and design preference. A typical size is ¼in (6mm) in diameter. Larger joints may benefit from heavier pegs, depending on the design.

BY HAND OR BY MACHINE

TOOLS NEEDED:

- Combination square
- Saddle square
- Marking gauge
- Bradpoint drill bit
- Hand drill or electric drill
- Dowel
- Awl
- Hammer
- Flush-trim saw

A drawbored mortise-and-tenon joint beefs up a traditional joint by using pegs or dowels to reinforce the joint and to prevent the pieces from separating. This works by slightly offsetting the hole in the tenon from that in the mortise. When the peg is driven in, this offset helps draw the joint tight.

1 Trace around the tenon on the mortised piece to help locate the mortise. The square helps hold the two pieces flush with one another as you mark the lines.

2 The layout lines on the mortised piece mirror the size and location of the desired mortise.

3 Transfer the marked lines to the edge of the workpiece where the mortise is to be formed. These lines define the length of the mortise.

4 Use the tenon to set the marking gauge to mark the cheeks or side walls of the mortise.

5 Referencing each face of the piece to be mortised, score the cheek lines with the marking gauge.

6 It's helpful to trace over the scored lines with a sharp pencil to make them more visible.

7 Cut the mortise using your preferred selection of tools and check the fit of the tenon. Make any adjustments necessary to achieve a snug fit.

8 You have a choice of the location and number of pegs for the joint. Here, I'm choosing to use one peg centered on the mortise.

9 Extend the peg's centerline around to the face of the mortised piece.

10 Use a combination square to mark consistent locations for the pegs from the edge of the workpiece. Be careful not to locate the hole too close to the bottom of the mortise or end of the tenon. This can cause a weak joint.

11 Mark the peg hole location with an awl to provide a registration point for the drill bit. Drill the holes using a bradpoint drill bit. You can choose to drill through the workpiece or only through one cheek of the mortise and partially into the other. The second method provides a neater appearance on the back side of the assembly.

12 Dry-fit the tenon into the mortise. Using the same bradpoint bit used to drill the hole, insert it into the hole and lightly tap it to mark a centerpoint on the tenon.

13 Disassemble the joint and note the dimple formed by the drill bit.

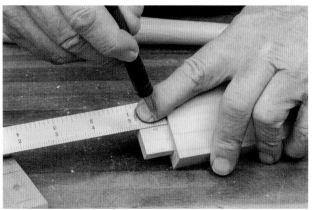

14 For a drawbore joint to work, the hole in the tenon must be offset toward the shoulder of the tenon. Mark a new centerpoint about 1/32in (0.8mm) from the dimple on the shoulder side.

15 Mark the new hole location with an awl and drill the hole through the tenon.

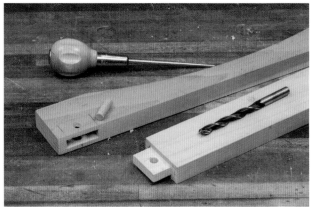

16 Cut lengths of dowel extra long to tap into the assembled joint, drawing the tenon tight into the mortise.

17 Before driving the peg in, slightly round over or taper one end with sandpaper to make driving it in easier.

18 Insert the peg into the hole in the assembled joint and firmly tap it until it bottoms out in the hole or the opposite face of the workpiece.

19 Use a flush-trim saw to cut the excess dowel close to the face of the assembled joint then sand smooth.

WORKSHOP NOTES

Basic tools for the drawbore joint.

WEDGED THROUGH TENON

A wedged mortise-and-tenon joint is a self-locking joint that proves strong and with an opportunity for some design embellishment. The joint features a through mortise that tapers slightly along its depth, making the mortise a bit longer on the outside of the joint than the inside. Many craftsmen take the opportunity to use a contrasting hardwood for the wedges to draw attention to the joint. You put a lot of effort into creating a strong joint. Why not draw attention to it and impress your friends and family with your craftsmanship?

Above: The tenon passes through the mortise with its end flush with the outer surface. Two saw kerfs near and parallel to the edges of the tenon accommodate wedges.

Far right: When the tenon is assembled into the mortise, hardwood wedges driven into the tenon's saw kerfs force the tenon to spread, locking it into the tapered mortise.

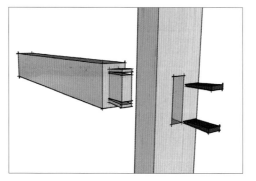

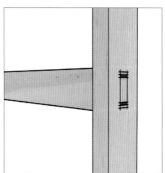

BY HAND

When designing a wedged through tenon joint, it's best to orient the wedges perpendicular to the grain direction in the mortised piece. If the wedges run parallel with the grain, the potential exists to split the mortised piece if the wedges are driven with too much force. You can orient the wedges in any direction—just be mindful of the grain direction as you tap the wedges into place.

1 Start by determining the thickness of the piece to be mortised. This provides a minimum dimension for the length of the through tenon.

2 Transfer this dimension to the tenon piece, marking all four sides. It doesn't hurt to add about 1/16in (1.5mm) to the length of the tenon so it will sit proud when assembled into the mortise. You'll plane or sand it flush after assembly.

3 Set the marking gauge to the desired width of the tenon shoulder, or cheeks of the tenon. This determines the final tenon width and thickness. It's easiest to keep this dimension consistent on all four sides of the tenon.

4 Mark the tenon cheeks all around from the baseline (shoulder) to the end of the workpiece.

5 Carry the lines around to the end of the workpiece. These lines serve as guides for the hand saw when cutting the tenon.

6 With the cutting edge of the chisel nestled in the scored line defining the tenon shoulder, make a few solid taps to deepen the line.

7 With the bevel down and the chisel edge about 1/16in (1.5mm) to 1/8in (3mm) to the waste side of the shoulder line, make a few taps to remove thin chips, creating a shallow V-groove.

8 With the teeth of the saw blade resting in the chiseled groove, cut the shoulders all around down to the cheek lines marked earlier.

9 Staying on the waste side (outside) of the layout lines, saw down to the shoulder to define the tenon.

10 Complete the tenon by sawing the face cheeks.

11 After the tenon is cut, make two saw kerfs to accommodate the wedges during assembly. Keep the kerfs fairly close to the sides of the tenon—about ¼in (6mm) to 3/8in (10mm) to ensure the wood will flex when the wedges are driven home.

12 On the workpiece to be mortised, locate the bottom of the mortise and mark it on opposite faces.

13 After cutting the tenon using your preferred method, use the tenon as a guide to mark the top of the mortise.

14 Extend the layout lines around the workpiece to the opposite face. For a clean, straight mortise through the workpiece, it's important that the layout lines on both faces align.

15 Mark the centerline down the length of the mortise.

16 Using the midpoint of the tenon as a reference, mark the width of the tenon onto the mortise layout. If you're handy with math, you can also use a marking gauge after taking into account the actual tenon thickness and width of the mortised piece.

17 Based on your tick marks for the thickness of the tenon, set the marking gauge to score the location of the mortise walls. Remember to do this on both faces.

18 Verify your layout lines with the tenon.

19 Use a chisel and mallet to deepen the lines defining the end of the mortise on both faces of the workpiece.

20 Use a straight block of wood as a chisel guide to define the side walls of the mortise. To avoid splitting, use light taps when the chisel's edge is oriented parallel to the wood grain.

21 Begin removing waste, being careful to stay within the layout lines.

22 Working from both ends of the mortise, keep scoring the walls of the mortise then removing thin chips. Work from both sides until the mortise is through the workpiece.

23 Use the chisel guide to clean up the walls of the mortise.

24 One of the main features of a wedged through tenon joint is the tapered mortise. There is a very slight taper from one side of the workpiece to the opposite side. Use a chisel guide cut at a slight angle to start paring the ends of the mortise from the outside. Place the chisel guide about 1/16in (1.5mm) from the end of the mortise. It doesn't take much of a taper to create a strong joint.

25 Cutting the wedges to fit the joint properly is an art that requires some practice. The wedge must be thick enough to force the side of the tenon to the end of the mortise. But it must be short enough so that it doesn't bottom out in the saw kerf before the tenon is secure. It will take some experimentation.

26 After applying glue and driving the wedges tight, use a flush-cut saw to trim the wedges. After the glue dries, sand or plane the end of the tenon flush.

BY MACHINE

TOOLS NEEDED:

- Tablesaw
- Mortiser or drill press and a Forstner bit
- Miter gauge
- Chisel

The layout work for marking the tenon and mortise is the same regardless of the tools you use to create them.

1 On your tablesaw, set the height of the saw blade to the width of the tenon shoulders. You won't be cutting through the piece, so it's okay to use the rip fence as a stop to define the length of the tenon while you push the piece using the miter gauge.

2 Cut the shoulder lines on all four sides, keeping the end of the workpiece tight against the fence.

3 Set the blade height to the shoulder of the tenon. Use a tenon jig to guide the workpiece to cut the cheek.

4 Rotate the workpiece 180° to cut the opposite cheek.

5 Adjust the position of the tenon jig to cut two saw kerfs for the wedges.

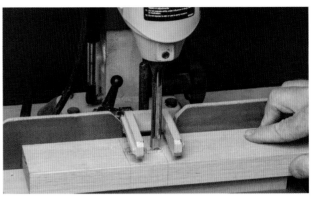

6 A mortiser is the perfect tool for creating accurate mortises. In the absence of a mortiser, use a drill press and a Forstner bit to drill out the majority of the waste then use a chisel to clean up the remainder.

7 Since the mortise is wider than the mortising chisel, align the chisel with one side of the mortise. Drill the end holes followed by overlapping holes in between. You'll be drilling through the workpiece, so place a piece of scrap under it to protect the bit as it exits the workpiece. Rotate the workpiece 180° to finish the other side of the mortise.

8 Follow the same steps as for the hand tool method to create the tapered mortise using a chisel guide and assembling the joint.

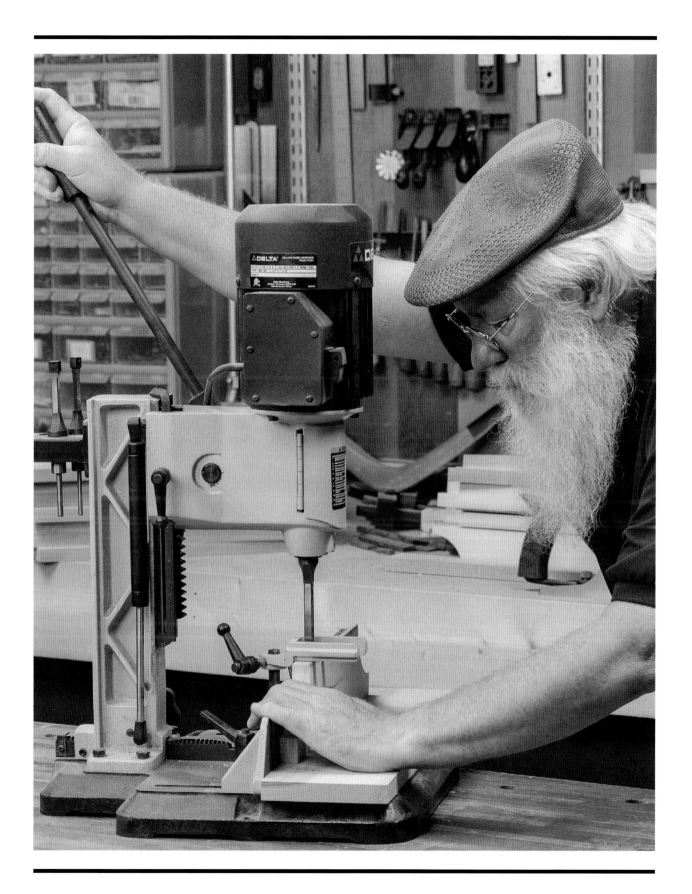

FLAT MITER JOINT

Miter joints are ubiquitous in picture frame and door construction. The most common variation of the miter joint is two pieces joined at right angles with a 45° cut at the end of each piece.

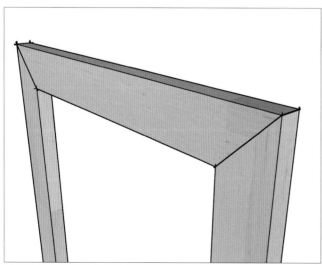

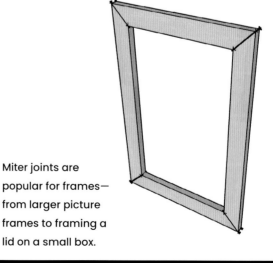

Miter joints are popular for frames— from larger picture frames to framing a lid on a small box.

BY HAND

TOOLS NEEDED:

- Miter square or combination square
- Clamps
- Hand plane
- Saw
- Shooting board
- Miter box

Cutting miters by hands requires only a few simple tools and some practice making smooth, straight cuts. A little cleanup with a hand plane or block sander results in gap-free joints.

1 An inexpensive miter box from the hardware store is perfectly suitable for rough-cutting miters. Slots in the sides of the miter box guide the saw for consistent cuts. Clamping the workpiece makes for cleaner cuts.

2 A plastic carpenter's square works well for laying out and cutting miters. The plastic won't damage saw teeth.

3 The trick with using a plastic carpenter's square for cutting miters is to securely hold the fence of the square tight to the workpiece. Clamping the square to the workpiece can help with this.

4 A shooting board guides a plane to trim the end of a workpiece perfectly smooth. A 45° fence screwed to the bed of the shooting board makes trimming and fine-tuning the fit of miters an easy task.

5 After cutting the miters, use a square to ensure the assembled joint is 90°.

6 Dry-fit the complete frame, make note of any gaps, no matter how small.

7 To trim a whisper-thin shaving from the heel or toe of the miter for a perfect joint, the shooting board (see box opposite) comes to the rescue.

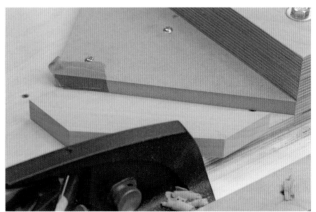

8 Masking tape makes a great shim to minutely adjust the angle of the workpiece for tweaking the fit of a joint.

SHOOTING BOARD WITH 45° FENCE

For its simple construction, a shooting board is a must-have in any workshop, whether you prefer to work with hand or power tools. There is no other tool

as precise as a hand plane for creating a glue-ready surface. A shooting board also excels at allowing you to tweak the fit of the workpieces for gap-free joints.

A basic shooting board consists of a flat bed with a solid fence. One side of the shooting board forms a track for a hand plane. A miter plane is shown here but any bench plane is suitable. The most critical aspect of the shooting board is that the fence must be absolutely square to the edge of the bed that forms the plane track. On this shooting board, strong bolts allow for minor adjustments to the fence yet still hold it in place securely.

Top: A basic shooting board squares off the ends of workpieces leaving a smooth surface.
Above: Adding a removable 45° fence to the shooting board enables the precise trimming of miters.

9 Here, the tape kicks the end of the workpiece out just a hair to trim the heel of the miter. Add layers of masking tape until the fit of the joint is perfect.

10 Instead of working with awkward clamps when gluing up miter joints, use a rub joint. Start by applying a thin layer of wood glue to the workpieces. Allow the glue to set for a few minutes. The end grain of the wood will soak up some of the glue. Apply a second thin layer of glue.

11 Firmly hold the joint together and rub the pieces back and forth to spread the glue evenly. As you rub, you'll quickly notice how the pieces become harder to move. At this point, make sure the pieces are in their proper position.

12 Once the pieces are aligned, hold the joint for about a minute then allow the glue to set for at least an hour. Modern glues make strong joints suitable for most applications.

BY MACHINE

TOOLS NEEDED:

- Miter gauge
- Stop block
- Tablesaw
- Auxiliary fence

You might think that the first choice for making miter joints with machines is with a miter (chop) saw. However, they're designed more for rough carpentry than fine joinery. A tablesaw makes it easier to make minor adjustments for professional miter joints.

1 The miter gauge on the tablesaw enables 45° cuts. Invest in a quality miter gauge accurately machined for the most precise angled cuts. Add an auxiliary fence to fully support the workpiece through the cut.

2 A stop block clamped to the miter gauge fence enables you to cut frame pieces at consistent lengths.

3 While firmly holding the workpiece against the miter gauge fence and stop block, slowly guide the workpiece through the cut. A quality crosscut saw blade yields smoother cuts.

SPLINED MITER JOINT

Spline joinery is useful for a variety of applications including frames, boxes, and furniture. The spline creates a strong mechanical connection between the two pieces and reinforces the joint while adding a decorative element.

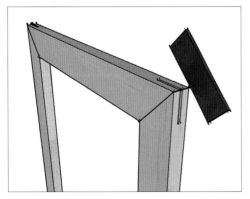

Each mating piece features a slot, or groove, that accepts a spline.

BY HAND

TOOLS NEEDED:

- Chisels
- Japanese saws
- Planes
- Marking gauge
- Marking knife

Making a splined miter joint with hand tools is easier than you might think. Just make a couple of cuts with a hand saw to create the slots followed by a narrow chisel to clean them up. Then you can cut a contrasting hardwood for the splines, planing them to fit the slot.

1 Start with a glued-up miter joint or frame (see pages 86–91). When cutting a slot with hand tools, select a chisel with the same desired width of the slot.

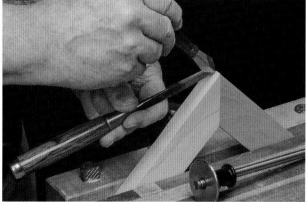

2 After laying out the position of the slot on the miter joint, use the chisel to mark the width of the slot with a marking knife.

3 Mark both sides of the chisel to lay out the width of the slot.

4 With a marking gauge, extend the layout lines for the slot width the entire length, or depth, of the slot.

5 Mark the depth of the slot. Make sure the slot isn't so deep that it cuts through the inside of the frame.

6 Use a hand saw with fine teeth to cut one side of the slot. Keep the layout lines in sight to help you guide the saw along the inside of the line.

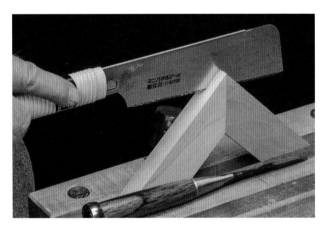

7 Cut the opposite side of the slot using the same technique.

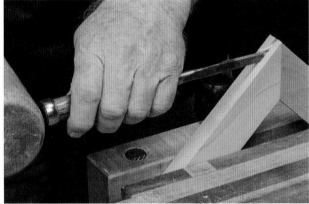

8 With the chisel you selected for the width of the slot, begin to remove small amounts of material between the two saw cuts.

9 Pare down to the marked depth of the slot.

10 The long grain of the spline should run perpendicular to the joint line for maximum strength. Cut the splines oversized then sand or plane them to thickness to fit snugly in the slot.

11 Check the fit of the spline often as you fine-tune the fit.

12 Once you're satisfied with the fit of the spline, apply a thin layer of glue and tap the spline into place.

13 After the glue dries, trim the excess spline then plane or sand it smooth.

14 A spline is a perfect way to add eye-catching detail to your work while adding strength to the miter joint.

WORKSHOP NOTES

JAPANESE DOZUKI SAW

A Japanese dozuki saw is a crosscut saw with fine teeth on a thin blade designed for detail work. Dozuki saws feature a steel spine on the back of the blade to keep it in tension and cutting straight during use. Available in a variety of lengths and different teeth per inch (TPI), they prove themselves invaluable in the workshop.

Japanese saws cut on the pull stroke in contrast with a push stroke common with Western-style saws. While it may take some getting used to, using a Japanese saw can improve your sawing accuracy.

Below: This small dozuki saw is perfect for detail work.

BY MACHINE

TOOLS NEEDED:
- Tablesaw
- Spline jig

For consistent joinery, cutting splined miter joints is best done with a jig at the tablesaw. The jig holds the mitered joint and positions it over the blade to create the slot.

1 A tablesaw makes quick work of cutting miters.

2 After a mitered joint is glued up, cut the spline on the tablesaw using a jig similar to the one shown here. This spline jig is designed to ride on the rip fence of the tablesaw. It features two fences positioned 45° to provide a resting place for the assembled frame or joint.

3 After positioning the rip fence to locate the slot on the miter joint, set the depth of the blade to match the slot depth. Run the jig across the blade with the mitered joint held firmly.

4 Repeat the process for the remaining joints. The spline jig makes the slots consistent.

5 Select stock for the splines and cut them to rough thickness and oversized in length and width. Plane or sand them to thickness to fit the slot.

BOX JOINTS

Box joints (also known as finger or comb joints) get their name from vintage packing crates and boxes. Mass-produced box joints are cut using special machinery for quick, easy, and strong assemblies.

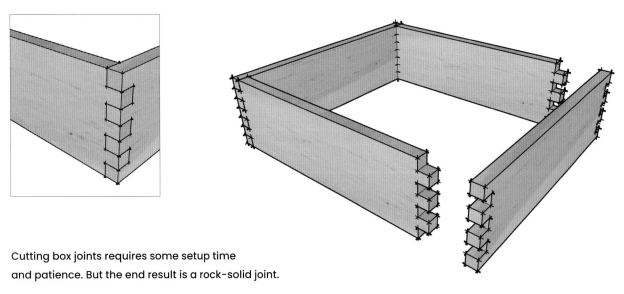

Cutting box joints requires some setup time
and patience. But the end result is a rock-solid joint.

BY HAND

TOOLS NEEDED:

- Marking gauge
- Dividers•
- Square
- Marking knife
- Saw
- Mallet
- Chisels
- Coping saw

Creating box joints by hand can be challenging but rewarding at the same time. All it takes is some practice with a saw and chisel. Hand-cut box joints also allow you to be creative with the spacing for a unique look.

1 The key to tight-fitting box joints is to first make sure the ends of the workpieces are perfectly square. Mark the orientation of all the workpieces and label the joints.

2 Set a marking gauge to just a bit over the thickness of one of the workpieces. This leaves the joints just a little high when assembled. You'll sand or plane them flush after assembly.

3 Using this setting of the marking gauge, mark the baseline of the box joint on each face of the workpieces.

4 Mark the baseline on the edge of one of the workpieces. The outside edges will be notched to accommodate the pin from the adjoining workpiece.

5 The width and number of pins and notches is a matter of personal preference. Use a pair of dividers to help you lay out the box joint features evenly across the end of the workpieces. For visual balance, make sure the outer edges of one of the workpieces features a full pin.

6 Use a marking knife and small square to score down to the baseline the lines that define the edges of the pins and notches.

7 For narrower workpieces, you can use the marking gauge to score the lines defining the pins and notches.

8 Extending the layout lines around to the end of the workpiece serves as a guide for the saw and chisel.

9 Trace over the scored lines and mark the waste areas to assist in visualizing how the joint will be assembled and serve as guides for the saw and chisel. Note the odd number of pins on one workpiece and an even number of pins on the adjoining piece.

10 With all the lines marked to verify the layout of the joint, you're ready to start cutting the notches.

11 With the saw on the waste side of the layout line, saw down to the baseline, keeping the saw as close to the scored line as possible.

12 For the workpiece with notches on the outer edges, saw along the baseline to remove the waste and create the notch.

13 Using a chisel width that matches the width of the notches, use a mallet to score the baselines of the notched areas, keeping the bevel of the chisel facing the waste.

14 With a piece of scrap under the workpiece, work to remove the waste from the notched areas by flipping the workpiece over and working from both sides.

15 Prying away the waste as you chisel the baseline deeper makes waste removal easy.

16 After sawing and removing the bulk of the waste with chisels, use the scored lines as guides to pare away any remaining material. The goal is smooth, square sides to the notches.

17 Clamping the workpiece in the vise makes it easier to control the chisel when paring away waste. Check the fit of the joint often to sneak up on a gap-free joint. Don't force the joint together. Too much pressure can split the workpiece.

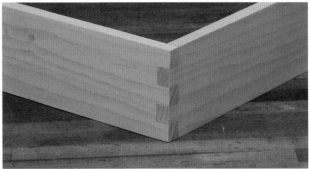

18 After test-fitting, apply glue and then sand the joint smooth after the glue dries.

BY MACHINE

TOOLS NEEDED:

By method:

A. Bandsaw
- Coping saw or fretsaw

B. Router table
- Straight router bit
- Clamp

The most popular method for creating box joints is to use a box-joint jig on the tablesaw (with a dado blade) or router table, as shown here. Another method requires some careful layout and cuts at the bandsaw followed by a little chisel work to make great-looking joints.

A. BANDSAW OPTION

1 A bandsaw makes quick work of sawing along the layout lines to define the notches.

2 Using a coping saw or fretsaw, remove the bulk of the waste for each notch, being sure not to saw below the scored baseline of the joint.

3 With the majority of the waste removed, it's an easy task to clean up the joint with sharp chisels.

B. ROUTER TABLE OPTION

1 A shop-made box joint jig is easy to assemble. It consists of a tall fence and a "key" that determines the spacing of the notches and pins. Here, we're using a router table. You can also use a tablesaw if it can access a dado blade to cut wide notches.

2 The first step in making a box joint jig is to clamp a wide board to the face of the miter gauge and make a pass over a straight bit. The size of the bit determines the width of the notches.

3 Make a key to fit snuggly in the notch. Move the fence so that the space between the router bit and key matches the diameter of the bit.

4 With the workpiece held vertically against the fence, butt the end against the key and make a pass over the bit to create the first notch. NOTE: Use cutoff pieces the same thickness as your project pieces to home in on a perfect fit of the joint.

5 Move the workpiece so that the notch you just cut fits over the key and make another pass.

6 Repeat the process across the end of the workpiece. Don't worry if there is a little material left over or the last notch isn't as wide as the others.

TIP

Start with extra-wide workpieces. This way, you can trim them to the exact width needed after cutting the joint to show evenly spaced and sized notches and pins across the joint.

8 Test the fit of the joint. You may need to adjust the distance from the bit to the key in small increments to get a good fit.

7 Trim the workpieces to width after cutting the box joint. Leave a full pin or notch at each edge of the workpiece.

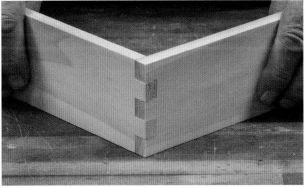

9 A properly fitting box joint should be snug, without gaps, and without needing to force the joint closed.

DOWEL JOINT

Dowel joinery is a simple, traditional joint used primarily for furniture construction but has many other applications as well.

Short hardwood dowels glued into holes in the mating pieces provide mechanical strength and additional glue surface for a strong joint.

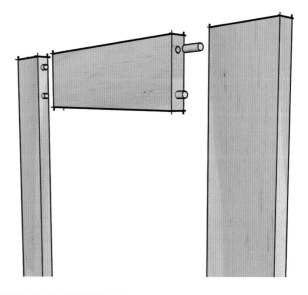

BY HAND

TOOLS NEEDED:

- Dowels
- Dowel centers
- Hand drill
- Portable electric drill
- Shooting board
- Edge plane
- Dowel centers
- Marking gauge
- Square
- Awl
- Bradpoint drill bit
- Straightedge ruler

Properly aligning the dowel holes becomes a challenge at times but with the right tools and techniques, it's not difficult.

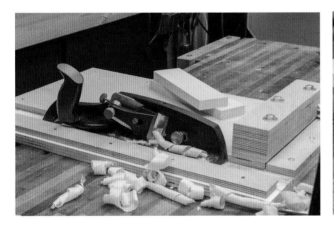

1 The key to square and tight dowel joints is ensuring the ends of the workpieces are perfectly square. A shooting board is a great tool for this task.

2 Labeling each joint and the faces of the workpieces is critical to avoid confusion later on. Here, I draw a line across the joint line to assist with proper orientation. A letter designation on each workpiece labels the joint.

3 To aid in aligning the dowels, use a square to draw lines at the dowel locations on each workpiece across the joint.

4 When drilling dowel into end grain, extend your marked lines around the end of the workpiece. A marking gauge makes this an easy, accurate task.

5 Likewise, extend the marked dowel lines around to the edge of the mating piece.

7 Dowels come in a variety of sizes. A common diameter for ¾in (19mm) stock is ¼in (6mm). Dowels feature ridges along their length to allow air to escape and provide room for excess glue.

8 Before drilling holes for the dowels, mark the centerpoints with an awl. This provides a registration point for the drill bit.

6 Use a marking gauge to mark the centerline of the thickness of each workpiece. It's important to reference the marked face of each piece to ensure the dowel holes align even if there is a minor variation of the thicknesses.

9 Use a small square to serve as a visual reference when drilling holes in one workpiece using a hand drill. This helps to keep the bit square to the surface in all directions. Of course, you can use a drill press to make this easy. Use a bradpoint bit for the best results.

10 Dowel centers make it easy to transfer the dowel locations to the adjoining workpiece. These steel or brass pins come in a variety of diameters.

11 One end of the dowel center fits snugly into the dowel hole. The projecting point transfers the center location to the mating piece.

12 Use a straightedge to keep the parts properly aligned while pressing them together. Use firm pressure to mark dimples in the workpiece.

13 After marking the mating piece with the dowel centers, make note of the dimples. Highlight them with a pencil, if necessary.

14 The dimples formed by the dowel centers become the registration point for drilling the dowel holes. Again, it's important to keep the drill bit square to the worksurface.

15 Insert dowels into one of the workpieces without glue and test the fit. Then you can add glue to the end of the dowels and mating surfaces of the joint.

16 Assemble the joint and apply clamps to draw the joint tight.

WORKSHOP NOTES

DOWEL JIG

A dowel jig is a simple mechanical device that provides a sure-fire way to locate and drill dowel holes. The jig fits over the workpiece with a fence on each side. As you tighten the jig, it automatically centers the jig on the thickness of the workpiece. On top of the jig, long-wearing, steel guide bushings serve to position the drill bit for accurate hole placement. Most jigs come with bushings to accommodate a variety of dowel diameters. These interchangeable bushings simply screw into the body of the jig.

Left: Accurate dowel hole placement is guaranteed when using a self-centering dowel jig. Above: Drill guide bushings fit into a range of hole locations and screw securely in place.

BY MACHINE

One of the handiest tools for creating dowel joints by machine is a doweling jig. There are dozens of jigs that make dowel joints using your hand drill, ranging from inexpensive to fancy, costly jigs. But all you need is a simple dowel jig to get great results.

1 Before using a dowel jig, read the instructions to determine recommended dowel spacing. Mark across the joint line at these locations.

2 This dowel jig features windows to assist in positioning it on the workpiece using your layout lines as a guide. Marks on the body of the jig align with the marks on the workpiece.

3 Insert guide bushings at the appropriate locations based on the layout lines. Use a portable drill with a bradpoint bit for clean, accurate dowel holes.

4 Dowels reinforce simple end-grain or butt joints for a super-strong assembly.

THROUGH DOVETAIL JOINT

The through dovetail joint provides mechanical strength. Pins formed on the end of one piece fit between dovetail-shaped fingers (tails) on the opposite piece. Properly constructed, the dovetail joint resists pulling apart in one direction.

Drawer fronts and backs are pin boards with the sides featuring the tails. You'll often find the dovetail joint in drawer, box, and cabinet construction.

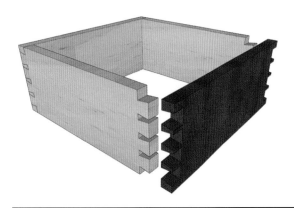 

BY HAND

TOOLS NEEDED:

- Saddle square
- Dovetail marker
- Marking gauge
- Marking knife
- Chisels
- Saws

There is a debate among woodworkers whether it's better to cut the tails first or pins first. My preference is to lay out and cut the tails first then use them to mark the pins. When laying out dovetails, you may run across ratios like "1:6" or "1:8." These define the slope, or angle, of the tail sides. A 1:6 ratio is a steeper angle than 1:8. Traditionally, 1:6 was used for softwoods while 1:8 was used for hardwood. With modern wood glues, the angle, size, and number of dovetails is mostly a matter of personal and creative design preferences.

1 As with most hand-cut joinery, start by marking the baseline. With through dovetails, the thickness of the adjoining piece defines the baseline. In this case, set the marking gauge to match the thickness of the pin board. When making a box, repeat this process on each end of the two tail boards.

2 Wrap the baseline around to the edges of the tail board.

TIPS

To avoid confusion later, label the pin and tail boards as well as the joints and the orientation of each board (in, out, up, or down).

If you're handy with one of many CAD programs available, you can experiment with the size and number of dovetails. Print out a template to use as a guide when laying out the dovetails on your project pieces. Get creative with your dovetail layout. You can vary the size, spacing, and number of dovetails to create an eye-catching design.

3 Lay out the desired number and size of the tails on the ends of the tail boards. The only limitation is the size of chisel used to remove the waste. Don't make the width of the waste area less than the width of your narrowest chisel. Here, I'm marking the edge of the first dovetail.

4 Reset the gauge to mark the line defining the width of the first dovetail.

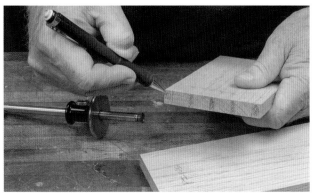

5 After defining the edges of all the tails, mark the waste area between them and at the edges of the tail board.

6 This dovetail marker acts as a saddle square by wrapping around the edge of a workpiece. The angled leg defines the angles of the tails. Align the square leg of the marker with the edges of the tails you marked on the end of the board.

> **TIP** If you don't own a dovetail marker, you can use a sliding bevel gauge to lay out the tails.

7 Mark the areas between the tails as waste to be removed. You'll also remove waste at the outer edges.

WORKSHOP NOTES

DOVETAIL MARKERS

Dovetail markers are a timesaver if you enjoy cutting dovetails by hand. Available in a variety of styles, most feature common dovetail slopes and a square fence for marking the ends of the tails. The thickness of these heavy-duty, aluminum dovetail markers provide a registration surface for a marking knife or pencil.

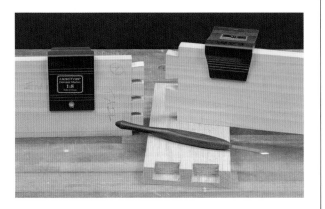

8 Use a saw to cut down the sides of the tails, making sure the saw stays on the waste side of the line. The trick here is to angle the saw blade to match the angle of the tail. It takes practice, but, in time, you'll be able to cut the tails quickly and accurately.

9 Cut down the opposite side of the tail, keeping an eye on the angle. Make sure not to cut past the baseline.

10 Repeat the process until the sides of all the tails are cut.

11 Flip the workpiece on its side to remove the waste at the outer edges of the tail board.

12 Repeat to cut the waste from the opposite edge.

13 You can use chisels to remove the waste but it becomes much easier if you first remove the bulk of the waste with a fret or coping saw.

14 Place the edge of the chisel just inside the baseline and use a mallet to chop the waste, flipping the board and working from both sides. A piece of scrap placed under the workpiece protects the benchtop from chisel gouges.

15 Remove the waste between the tails, place the cutting edge in the scribed baseline, and chop down to create a clean, straight baseline. Work from both faces of the workpiece.

16 The tails will fit much better if the edges of the tails are square to the faces of the workpiece.

17 With the pin board clamped in the bench vise, support the back end of the tail board. It's common practice to use a hand plane placed on its side.

18 Making sure the tail board is parallel to the benchtop, securely hold the tail board flush with the outer face and edges of the pin board. Trace the shape of the tails with a marking knife.

19 Work across the tail board while holding it securely to prevent movement.

20 Use a conventional square or the straight leg of a dovetail marker to extend the marked pin lines down to the baseline on each face of the pin board.

21 Use care to mark the proper areas for the waste. More than one woodworker has miscut a pin board by removing the wrong waste.

22 Cutting the pins requires aligning the saw blade with the angle of the pin side while cutting straight down to the baseline.

23 Work across the pin board, being sure to keep the saw on the waste side of the line.

24 Use a fret or coping saw to remove the bulk of the waste between the pins.

25 Remove the waste between the pins using a sharp chisel. Note that the waste area is wider on one side of the pin board than the other.

26 Finish cleaning up the sockets down to the baseline.

27 Test the fit of the joint. You may have to pare the pins or tails to remove high spots if the joint is too tight. The more you practice, the less trimming you'll have to do. I intentionally left the joints proud to sand or plane smooth.

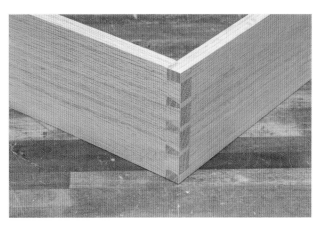

28 The completed, sanded through dovetail joint shows off your craftsmanship.

BY MACHINE

TOOLS NEEDED:

- Saddle square
- Dovetail marker
- Marking gauge
- Marking knife

By method:

A. Bandsaw
- Bandsaw

B. Handheld router
- Dovetail jig

Gap-free dovetail joints are the hallmark of a craftsman. Cutting the tails with a bandsaw is a quick way to get started. A dovetail jig with a handheld router is worth the investment for multiple, uniform joints.

A. BANDSAW

1 A bandsaw makes cutting the tails quick and easy. Just remember to cut on the waste side of the layout lines.

2 Work your way across the end of the tail board, rotating the workpiece with each cut to follow the angle of each tail.

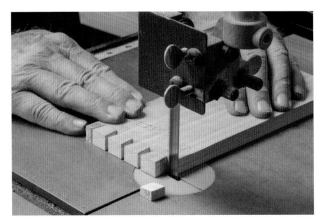

3 With the sides of the tails cut, you'll still need to do some hand work with chisels to clean up the waste in between the tails. Cut the waste away from the edges of the workpiece, paying careful attention to avoid cutting over the baseline.

4 Using a bandsaw beats using a hand saw for speed yet the end result is the hand-cut look so desirable in fine woodworking.

B. ROUTER AND DOVETAIL JIG

1 A dovetail jig eliminates the saw and uses a handheld router instead. With a proper setup, the router makes quick work of cutting dovetails.

2 Most dovetail jigs feature a template with one side designed to cut the tails using a dovetail bit. Use a straight bit with the opposite side of the template to cut the pins. The router features a bushing that rides against the template to cut the pins or tails.

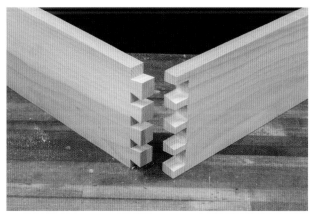

3 Check the fit of the dovetail joint and make any necessary adjustments before cutting your project parts. Keep the owner's manual within easy reach to get professional results from your dovetail jig.

TONGUE-AND-GROOVE

Tongue-and-groove joints are like edge joints (see pages 16–19) except that the pieces are joined using a tongue on one piece that fits into a groove on the mating piece. The mechanical connection helps keep the pieces aligned during final assembly.

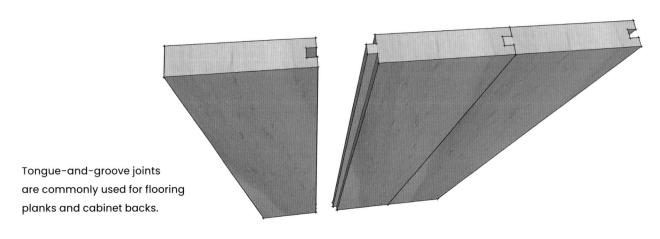

Tongue-and-groove joints are commonly used for flooring planks and cabinet backs.

BY HAND

Creating tongue-and-groove joints with hand tools is best done with special-purpose planes. A plow plane or combination plane allows you to use a wide variety of blades for various joinery and decorative applications. One of the blades creates a tongue on the edge of a workpiece. A complementary straight blade creates a groove precisely sized to accommodate the tongue.

Tongues are formed by creating a rabbet along two edges of a workpiece, leaving a tongue in the middle. A plane especially designed to cut rabbets, like the No. 78 duplex rabbet plane, excels at quickly creating a tongue.

CUTTING THE GROOVE

1 To use a plow plane, first adjust the position of the blade to center it on the edge of the workpiece. Do this by moving the fence. Set the height of the depth stop to create the desired groove depth. Start planing at the far end of the board with short strokes while firmly holding the fence against the face of the workpiece. Make each stroke a little longer, working your way back toward the near end.

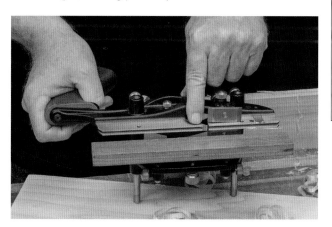

2 A pair of skates guide the straight blade to create the groove.

WORKSHOP NOTES

THE PLOW PLANE AND RABBETING PLANE

You can find vintage plow, combination, and rabbeting planes but new ones feature better materials and machining, making them a worthwhile investment.

A plow plane (left) accepts a variety of blades, including the tongue-and-groove blades shown. The No. 78 duplex rabbeting plane (right) makes quick work of cutting a pair of rabbets to form a tongue.

3 Make continuous strokes along the length of the workpiece.

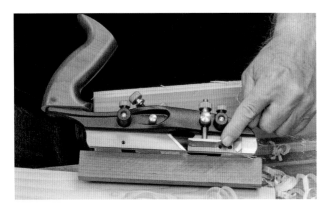

4 The depth stop sets the depth of the groove.

5 Continue planing until the blade fails to remove a shaving when the depth stop contacts the workpiece.

FORMING THE TONGUE

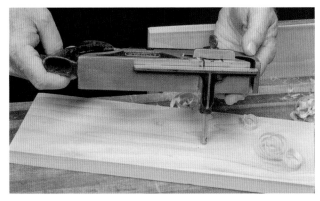

6 Set the position of the fence to create the desired width of the two rabbets that form a tongue. Adjust the depth for the depth of the rabbets.

7 Start at the far end of the workpiece with short strokes, holding the fence firmly against the face.

8 Make longer strokes while working back toward the near end of the workpiece. When the depth stop contacts the board, the plane stops cutting. Flip the workpiece 180° and repeat the process on the opposite edge, forming the tongue.

BY MACHINE

TOOLS NEEDED:

By method:

A. Router table

- ¼in straight cutter
- Spiral upcut bit

B. Tablesaw

The two most popular power tools for making tongue-and-groove joints are a tablesaw and router table. The tablesaw requires a little more setup and testing while the router table, with the right bit, provides great results, as well.

A. ROUTER TABLE

A router table equipped with a straight bit provides a quick and accurate method for creating tongues and grooves. Start with a straight bit slightly smaller in diameter than the desired groove width. You'll make two passes to form the groove, rotating the workpiece with each pass to center the groove on the edge.

1 A ¼in (6mm) diameter straight bit is perfect for routing grooves in ¾in (20mm) thick stock. Visually align the edge of the workpiece centered on the bit. The exact width of the groove doesn't matter—you'll make the tongues to fit later.

TIP

When machining tongue-and-groove joints, think of it in an assembly line fashion. For example, with each routing or tablesaw operation and to get consistent results, run all your project pieces through at the same setting. Then adjust for the next cut and run all the pieces through. Repeat until all the joints are complete.

2 Make a pass over the bit. A spiral upcut bit removes chips quickly.

3 Rotate the workpiece 180°.

4 Make another pass to center the groove on the width of the workpiece.

5 Switch to a ½in (13mm) or larger straight router bit to create the tongue.

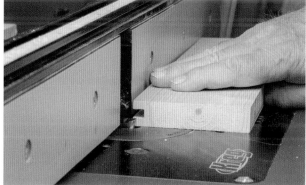

6 Adjust the height of the bit to just below the inside wall of the groove. It's best to start too low and gradually increase the height of the bit to sneak up on a perfect fit in the groove. Adjust the fence so that the distance to the outside edge of the bit matches the depth of the groove.

7 Make a pass over the bit to create one rabbet.

8 Flip the workpiece end over end and make another pass to form a tongue.

9 Check the fit of the tongue in the groove. Aim for a snug fit that doesn't require excess force to draw the joint together.

10 If the tongue is too wide to fit into the groove, raise the bit very slightly and make two passes as before on each side of the workpiece.

11 Check the fit and make any adjustments necessary until the joint goes together smoothly.

B. TABLESAW

While a dado blade on the tablesaw is an appropriate approach to creating tongue-and-groove joints, safety regulations outside the United States prohibit the use of dado blades. Instead, you can accomplish the task with a single blade.

1 Set the blade height to the desired groove depth. Start by visually aligning the workpiece close to the center of the workpiece thickness and make a pass.

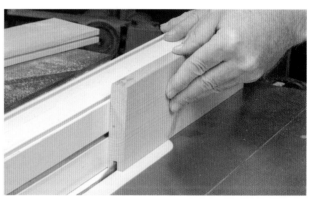

2 Rotate the workpiece 180° and make another pass. This keeps the groove centered.

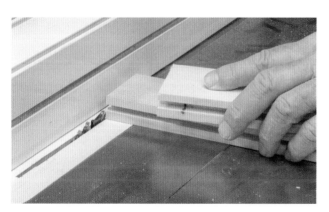

3 With the grooves cut on all the workpieces, adjust the blade height to just below the inside wall of the groove. Set the distance of the rip fence from the outside of the blade equal to the groove depth.

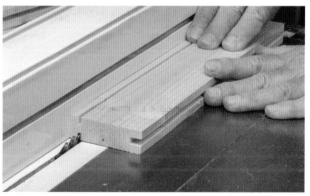

4 Make a pass over the blade, flip the workpiece end over end, and repeat the cut.

5 Adjust the position of the rip fence so the inside edge of the blade aligns with the outside wall of the groove.

6 Flip the workpiece to the tongue edge and make a pass to form one side of the tongue. Rotate the board 180° and cut the opposite side of the tongue. You may need to adjust the blade height to create clean, crisp corners at the bottom of the groove shoulders.

7 Note that the saw is configured so the waste falls to the outside of the blade, thus preventing kickback.

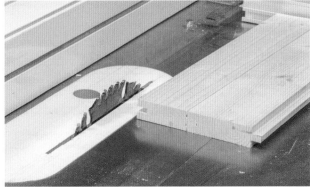

8 A properly fit tongue-and-groove joint should only require gentle pressure to assemble.

WEDGED THROUGH (TUSK) TENON

A variation of the traditional mortise-and-tenon joint, a wedged through tenon, also called a tusk tenon, utilizes a wedge to hold the tenon workpiece into the mortised piece where the mortise is open on both sides.

The tenon passes all the way through the mortise and features a tapered slot for housing the wedge. The wedge pulls the joint tight for a rock-solid assembly.

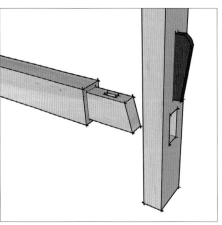
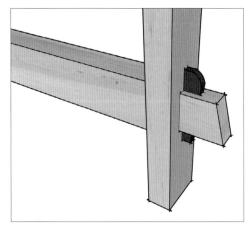

BY HAND

TOOLS NEEDED:

- Chisels
- Saws
- Saddle square
- Marking knife
- Marking gauge
- Small square
- Forstner bit
- Mallet
- Clamps

This joint is used for knock-down furniture since it can be assembled and disassembled easily. Or it can simply serve as a decorative—more than functional—feature for your project.

1 The first step in making a tusk tenon joint is to form the open mortise. Layout work is critical to make sure the mortise aligns on both faces of the workpiece.

2 After marking the length of the mortise on the face of the workpiece, use a saddle square to extend the lines around to the edges.

3 Continuing those lines around to the opposite face, mark the ends of the mortise.

4 Start by defining the ends of the mortise using a chisel. With the bevel facing the waste, make a couple of firm taps with a mallet to cleanly define the mortise. If needed, use a small square to ensure square mortise walls all the way through the workpiece.

5 Using the same chisel with the bevel down, remove a small chip at each end of the mortise.

6 Use a wide chisel to define the cheeks of the mortise. Use care when tapping with a mallet. It's easy to split the workpiece along the grain if too much force is used.

7 With the outer edges of the mortise defined on the front and back, drill out the waste with a Forstner bit.

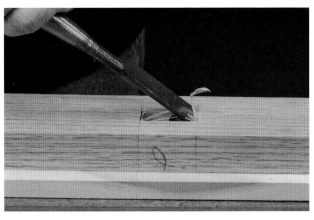

8 Use chisels to square up the mortise and remove the remaining waste.

WORKSHOP NOTES

A saddle square is such a simple, inexpensive tool that has so many uses in the workshop. It's designed to make it easy to transfer or extend layout lines around the corner of the workpiece. Use a marking knife or sharp pencil to mark the lines while holding the saddle square tight to the workpiece.

9 One trick to ensuring square walls on the mortise is to use a chisel guide. Here, a thick piece of wood is clamped to align with the layout line defining the mortise wall. This provides a reference surface for the back of the chisel to keep the walls square to the face of the workpiece.

10 Lay out the tenon on the mating workpiece. Make it extra-long for trimming after the wedge is fitted. Keeping the tenon too short can cause the end to split if the wedge is forced into the slot. It's best to leave plenty of material.

11 Mark the shoulder of the tenon using a square.

12 Use a saddle square (see box opposite) to extend the lines around to the edges.

13 Using the mortise size as a guide, mark out the side cheeks of the tenon using a marking gauge wrapping the line around the end of the workpiece.

14 Mark the face cheeks in a similar manner.

15 After laying out the tenon and marking the waste areas, visually check your lines against the mortise. In the end, you want the tenon to fit snugly into the mortise, but not so tight that you need to force it. Cut the shoulders and cheeks of the tenon using your preferred choice of tools (see pages 53–57 for advice on cutting tenons by hand).

16 Insert the tenon into the mortise, ensuring the shoulders of the tenon are tight against the mortised piece. Mark around the tenon to accurately locate the slot for the wedge.

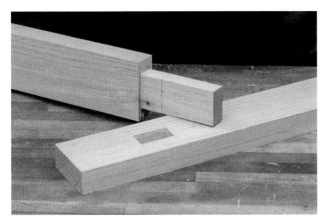

17 To ensure the wedge fits tight and draws the tenon securely to the mortised piece, offset the marked line about 1/32in (8mm) or so toward the shoulder of the tenon. This places the slot in the tenon just slightly inside the mortise.

18 Begin laying out the tapered slot. The slot is longer at the top of the tenon than the bottom. The amount of taper is mostly a matter of personal preference. A shallow taper makes it more challenging to fit the wedge but a wide taper removes too much material for the tenon, making it weak. Here, the taper is ¼in (6mm) longer at the top of the tenon than the bottom.

19 Mark the length of the tapered notch on the bottom of the tenon.

20 Use the marking gauge to mark the midline of the tenon to center the slot. Do this at the top and bottom of the tenon.

TIP

It's easy to find the centerline or midpoint on the face or edge of a workpiece using a marking gauge—without measuring. Extend the gauge until it's approximately at the distance from the edge of the workpiece to the center. It doesn't need to be exact. With the fence of the marking gauge tight to the face of the workpiece, make a small mark. Flip the marking gauge to the opposite side and make another small mark referencing that edge. If the two marks align, you've found the center. If not, simply make minor adjustments to the marking gauge and repeat the process until the marks align.

ABOVE: From the centerline, measure and mark the width of the slot for the wedge.
For the most strength, keep the slot width at one-third the thickness of the tenon or less.

21 For a visual indication of the size of the slot, mark the waste area.

22 Also mark the waste to be removed at the bottom of the tenon.

23 Using the marked lines that define the length of the slot at the top and bottom of the tenon, draw a line on the cheek of the tenon. This is the taper of the slot.

24 With the slot size and taper clearly marked, you'll use these lines to cut the mortise creating the slot.

25 Start by clamping the workpiece to the bench with a piece under the tenon to support it. Use a chisel to define the ends of the slot and begin removing the waste, aligning the chisel with the marked taper line.

26 Slowly keep working at removing the waste while keeping the slope of the taper in mind.

27 Use sharp chisels to clean up the walls of the tapered slot.

28 Try to keep the chisel aligned with the marked taper line as you clean up the inside walls of the slot.

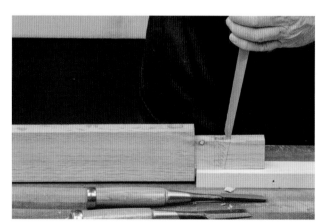

29 Keep working down, removing waste to about the halfway point.

30 Flip the workpiece over and use the same process to remove the remaining waste.

31 Test fit the tenon in the mortise and verify that the back side (straight side) of the slot sits just behind the face of the mortised piece.

32 A small bevel gauge is ideal for setting the angle to lay out the shape of the wedge.

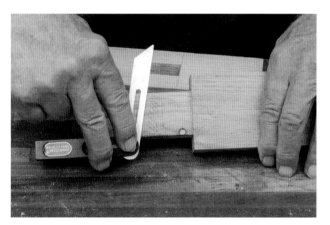

33 Reference the edge of the tenon and set the gauge to match your marked taper line.

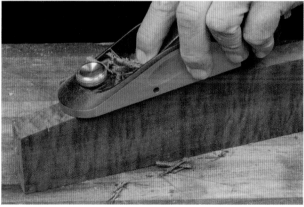

34 Plane a piece of hardwood to match the width of the tapered slot. Using the bevel gauge setting from before, mark a line then cut the wedge to rough shape. Use a hand plane to smooth the edges and make the taper straight.

35 Trim the wedge as needed to fit the tapered slot. The wedge should extend above and below the tenon. This can be a slow process as you repeatedly test the fit but your patience will be rewarded with a tight-fitting wedge.

36 Many craftsmen choose to embellish the top of the wedge with an eye-catching detail. Here, I simply rounded over the top, outside corner.

37 Before final sanding and finishing, cut the tenon to final length. For visual interest, I tapered the end of the tenon. With a few strokes of a small block plane, I chamfered the edges of the tenon.

38 Assemble the joint and lightly tap the wedge into place with a soft mallet. If the joint draws tight and you're pleased with the result, disassemble the joint, do any final sanding, and apply a finish.

BY MACHINE

TOOLS NEEDED:

- Tablesaw
- Bandsaw
- Mortiser
- Clamp

Making a tusk tenon joint starts with an extra-long tenon that extends through the mortise leaving ample material for the wedge (tusk). Cutting the tenon follows along the same lines as other tenon joints. The tapered through mortise for the wedge will still require a little hand work for a perfect fit.

1 After laying out the shoulders of the tenon, set the height of the tablesaw blade to cut the wide shoulders first.

2 Adjust the height of the saw blade, if necessary, to cut the side shoulders of the tenon. From here, you can use a bandsaw to remove the waste to complete the tenon.

3 A mortiser is great for removing the bulk of the waste from the tapered slot. Orient the workpiece with the small end of the slot facing up then align the bit to the layout line and drill through. Note the piece of scrap under the tenon to prevent blowout or chipping as the bit exits the workpiece.

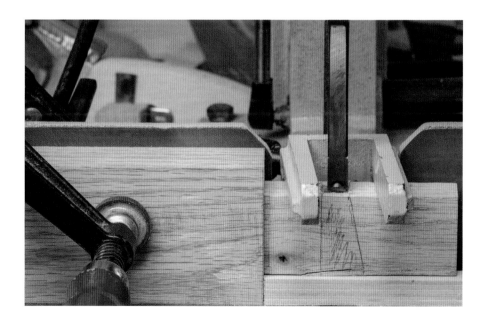

HALF-BLIND DOVETAIL

A half-blind dovetail joint is commonly used on drawer construction where a strong joint is desired but must be hidden. For example, many drawers feature fronts made from attractive veneer or expensive hardwood.

Below: The dovetailed portion of the joint fits into sockets cut on the end of the drawer front. Only the dovetailed portion of the joint is visible from the side. The joint is hidden when viewed from the front, hence the term "half-blind."

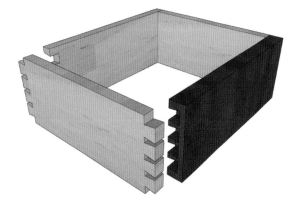

Below: It's not uncommon for half-blind drawer construction to feature a drawer front that is thicker than the sides. This facilitates making a strong joint with enough thickness to hide the joint when viewed from the front.

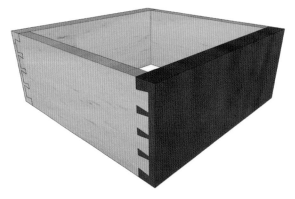

BY HAND

TOOLS NEEDED:

- Marking gauge
- Saddle square
- Small sliding bevel gauge
- Marking knife
- Chisels
- Mallet
- Japanese saw
- Hand plane
- Square

Cutting a half-blind dovetail joint will stress your skills with a hand saw and chisel. But with a little practice, you'll get the hang of it, creating great-looking joinery.

1 The first order of business when making a half-blind dovetail joint is to label the pieces.

2 To mark the baseline on the socket piece (a drawer front, for example), set the marking gauge to the thickness of the side.

3 Transfer this thickness measurement to the ends of the socket board. Reference off the inside face.

4 At the same setting, mark the baseline on the tail piece.

5 Also mark the baseline for the sockets.

6 Lay out the spacing and number of dovetails. Here, I'm marking the outside edges of the first tail. Make this mark from both edges to keep their size and location consistent.

7 A dovetail marker, such as this saddle square, features dovetail angles (slopes) on one leg of the square.

8 The sides on the adjacent leg of the square are at right angles to the edge of the workpiece in use.

9 In the absence of a dedicated dovetail marker, a small sliding bevel gauge makes a good substitute.

10 Set the blade of the bevel gauge to the desired dovetail angle, rest the stock of the gauge on the end of the workpiece, then trace along the blade down to the baseline to define the tails.

11 After extending the bar of the marking gauge, mark the inside edge of the first tails from each side of the workpiece.

12 With the straight leg of the dovetail marker aligned with the marks on the end of the tail board, trace along the angled edge on the face of the workpiece using a marking knife. To make the scored lines easier to see, trace over them with a thin pencil.

13 Slide the dovetail marker to align with the next mark. Note that you alternate drawing on each side of the marker to define the shape of the dovetails.

14 Continue marking across the workpiece, making sure the lines align with your layout marks on the end.

15 If you haven't done so already, mark the baseline at the edges of the tail board.

16 After completing the layout of the tails, mark the waste area between them as well as the two outer notches at the edges.

17 Before cutting the tails, verify the layout. All the baselines and tails should be clearly marked.

18 With the saw blade perpendicular to the face of the tail board, angle it right or left to follow the angle of the dovetail side. Make sure to cut on the waste side of the line.

19 Adjust the position and angle of the saw blade to cut the opposite side of the tail.

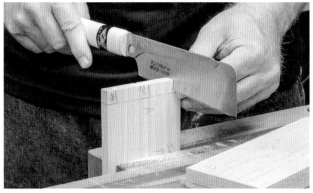

20 When cutting the sides of the tails, only cut down to the baseline marked on opposite faces.

21 Turn the workpiece on its side to cut the waste at the edges to form notches.

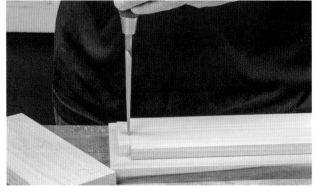

22 Using a chisel the same width as the distance between the tails at their narrowest, score the waste area with a few firm mallet taps.

23 Use a narrower chisel from the end of the tail board to pry up thin layers of waste. Repeat the process, flipping the workpiece over and working to remove the waste from both sides.

24 To ensure a gap-free joint, check that the edges of the tails are square to the faces of the board.

25 Place the socket (pin) board in the vise and align the top edge with a support such as a hand plane on its side.

26 Position the tail board on top of the plane and socket board. It should be parallel with the benchtop.

27 Align the baseline shoulders of the tail board with the inside face of the socket board. The ends of the tails should align with the baseline you marked on the end of the socket board.

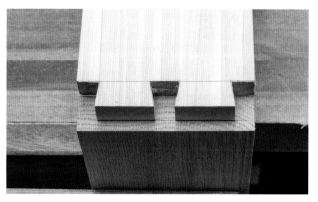

28 Verify the front-to-back position of the tail board, making sure it's centered on the width of the boards.

29 Holding the tail board firmly with downward pressure, trace the outline of the tails using a marking knife.

30 After marking both sides of each tail, trace over the scored lines with a thin pencil to make sawing and chiseling the waste easier.

31 Extend down to the baseline on each face the lines defining the edges of the tails. You can use a conventional square or saddle square for this task.

32 Mark the tail areas on the end of the socket board as waste to be removed.

33 With the socket board's inside face toward you, angle the saw and cut down to the baseline on the end and face of the board. This is a little tricky because the cut is square across the top but the blade is tilted to match the angle of the tail. A little practice goes a long way.

34 When sawing for half-blind dovetails, it's important to cut only to the two baselines. Overcuts will be visible in the finished joint.

35 After making the last cut for the sockets, you're ready to remove the waste and fit the tail board.

36 Use a wide chisel with a mallet to score the bottom of the socket just inside the marked baseline.

37 Begin removing waste in thin layers with a chisel and mallet.

38 Alternate cutting down the base of the socket and removing waste from the end.

39 Remove the waste in thin layers to avoid damaging the clean edges of the sockets.

40 As you work, you will eventually reach the corners where the saw could not reach. Use a chisel to carefully clean up the side walls of the sockets.

41 When using a mallet on a chisel with its cutting edge oriented with the grain, avoid using too much force as that could split the workpiece.

42 Remove the waste until you almost reach the baseline scored on the end of the workpiece.

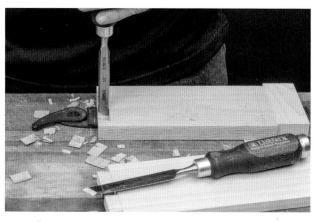

43 A skew chisel is a great tool for reaching into corners. Otherwise, a narrow chisel can be just as effective.

44 Clamp the workpiece in the bench vise and carefully pare down to the baseline. As you get close, you can set the cutting edge of the chisel in the scored baseline to reach final depth for the socket.

45 Finish cleaning up the sockets, particularly in the corners.

46 Test the fit of the tails in the sockets. You may need to pare away some high spots. Use good judgment and work slowly to avoid creating gaps in the joint.

47 A great-fitting half-blind dovetail joint is a testament to your craftsmanship.

WORKSHOP NOTES

SPECIALTY CHISELS

Sometimes, having the right tool for the task at hand can save hours of frustration. In the workshop, specialty chisels can be one of those tools. Dovetail chisels (center) get their name from their intended use. Unlike conventional, common bevel-edge bench chisels, dovetail chisels feature a sharp, thin edge, excellent for getting into tight areas.

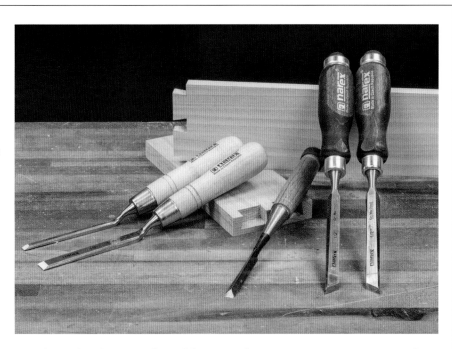

Skew chisels (right) feature an angled cutting edge. Available in left and right versions, the sharp point on a skew chisel can reach into areas no other chisel can.

Chisels with an offset handle (left) are sometimes called dog-leg or cranked-neck chisels. The handle is positioned behind and above the blade to provide clearance for your fingers. One use for these chisels is cleaning out dadoes and grooves across a wide workpiece where the handle on a standard chisel would interfere.

BY MACHINE

A dovetail jig, in combination with a handheld router, makes routing half-blind dovetails quick and easy. All it takes is a little setup work and testing to get perfect joints. Dovetail jigs are especially handy for making multiple dovetailed assemblies for a project.

When routing half-blind dovetails, the socket (pin) board clamps to the top of the jig while the tail board sits vertically underneath. One pass of a router equipped with a dovetail bit routs both the tails and the sockets.

1 The instructions that come with your dovetail jig show you how to properly orient the workpieces. The socket board is clamped horizontally with the tail board butting up against it in a vertical orientation.

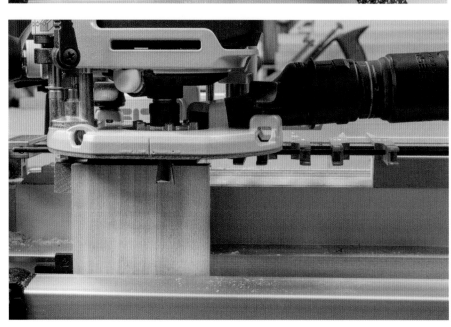

2 Set the cutting depth of the router bit according to the owner's manual. This is a starting point. You may have to make small adjustments for a properly fitting joint.

3 A guide bushing installed on the router's base follows the template to make the cuts in the two boards.

4 As you rout the tails, you also create the sockets for the tails to fit into.

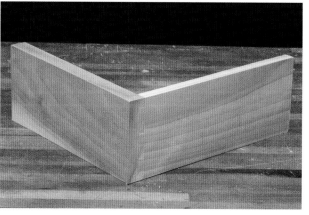

5 With a dovetail jig and a handheld router, your shop becomes a mini production facility for making multiple dovetail assemblies quickly and accurately.

STUB TENON AND GROOVE

Stub tenon and groove joinery creates strong cabinet door frames surrounding a panel. The joint gets its name from the short, stubby tenon at the ends of the rails. These fit into the grooves cut on the inside edge of the frame pieces to hold the panel. Stub tenon joinery relies on a good fit without gaps and modern wood glue to provide a strong joint.

Grooves cut on the inside edges of the frame pieces fit the door panel. Short tenons on the ends of the rails fit into the grooves.

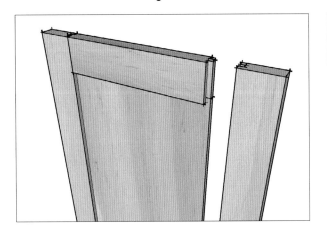

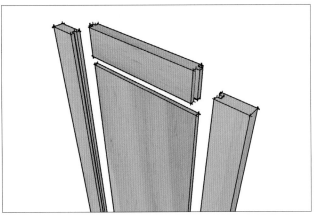

BY HAND

Stub tenons are easy to make by machine or by hand. The process starts with cutting a groove along one edge of long stock you'll use to make the frame. It's usually best to use machinery for this based on the lengths needed and consistency of groove size required. (See the Tongue-and-Groove joint on pages 122–131 to learn a couple of ways of cutting grooves.) Size the groove to match the door panel thickness. Now cut the stiles (vertical frame members) to final length. Measure the depth of the groove and take that into account when cutting the rails to length. With a little practice, you'll be building your own cabinet doors in no time.

1 With grooves cut in the frame stock, cut the pieces to length. To determine the length of the stub tenons, measure the depth of the groove with a marking gauge.

2 Transfer this measurement to the ends of the rails, marking the two wide faces.

3 Mark the grooved edge.

4 With the cutting edge of a chisel positioned on the scribed line, make a few firm taps with a mallet to deepen the line.

5 Follow the same procedure on the grooved edge. These marks indicate saw lines for cutting the stub tenon.

6 Place the chisel in the waste area with the bevel down and about 1/16in (1.5mm) to 1/8in (3mm) from the layout line. Make a few taps to remove narrow chips, creating a small V-groove.

7 Repeat the process with the grooved edge.

8 The thickness of the groove wall matches the shoulder depth for the stub tenon. Set the marking gauge to this distance.

9 Mark the ends of the rails to indicate where to saw the cheeks of the tenons.

10 Flip the workpiece over and mark the opposite cheek line.

11 On the edge opposite the groove, only mark the cheek lines from the shoulder line to the end of the workpiece. This edge is visible in the final assembly.

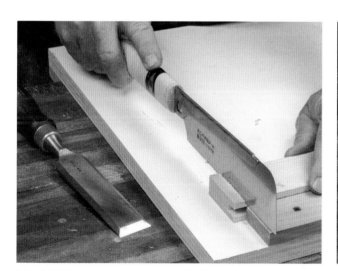

12 To saw the shoulders of the stub tenon, place the teeth of the saw in the V-notch you created with a chisel earlier.

13 Saw down to the cheek line you marked before.

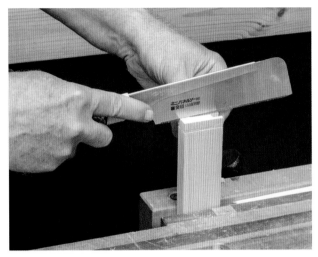

14 Clamp the workpiece in a bench vise to cut the cheeks down to the shoulder. Use care when starting the cut to keep the saw on the waste side of the line but as close to it as possible.

15 Rotate the workpiece 180° and cut the other cheek.

16 Check the fit of the stub tenon in the groove. Make any adjustments with a small shoulder plane until the tenon fits tight.

17 Dry-assemble the joint (without glue). The tenon should be snug but not too tight. Forcing a tight joint can split the groove walls. It's okay to have a small gap between the end of the stub tenon and the bottom of the groove. This provides some glue relief to allow the joint to close tightly.

BY MACHINE

When using a router table to create stub tenon and groove joints, the first order of business is to cut the groove in all of the stock that has been ripped to its final width.

1 Use a straight bit in the router table to create a groove. Use a bit diameter slightly less than the desired width of the groove. Make a pass then rotate the workpiece 180° and make another pass. This automatically centers the groove. Make minor adjustments to the fence position to home in on the target groove width.

2 To set up for cutting the stub tenon on the ends of the frame rails, adjust the height of the router bit until it's almost flush with the inside groove wall, as shown. You'll sneak up on the perfect tenon thickness to fit the groove by gradually raising the bit.

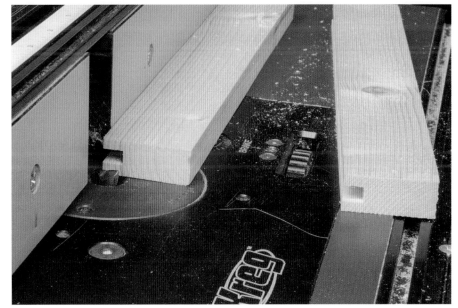

3 When routing the ends of a workpiece, use a wide backer board such as the plywood shown here. It keeps the workpiece square to the fence and backs up the cut as the bit exits, leaving a cleaner cut on the back side of the rail.

4 While securely holding the workpiece against the front edge of the backer board and against the fence, run the rail across the bit until it just cuts into the backer.

5 You're likely to see a small sliver of wood remaining. This is an indication that the tenon will be too thick, but you'll address that later.

6 Flip the rail over and make a pass on the other side.

7 Check the fit of the tenon in the groove on another piece. It should be a snug fit without gaps. If the tenon is too thick, raise the router bit a very small amount and make two more passes.

8 Check the fit of the tenon. If all is well, you can rout the tenons on the remaining rails.

9 In a typical frame assembly for cabinet doors, the rails are the horizontal members that fit into the vertical stiles.

10 After dry-fitting the pieces, all you need to do is fit the door panel in the frame and apply a dab of wood glue with slight clamping pressure to hold the stub tenon and groove joints together until the glue sets.

FLOATING (LOOSE) TENON

Like dowel joinery, a joint constructed using a floating, or loose, tenon is common in furniture and cabinet construction. A floating tenon piece fits into matching mortises in the two mating pieces to create a strong joint.

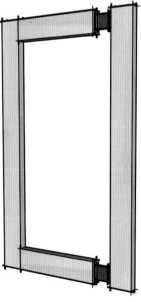

In many ways, loose tenon joinery is quicker to construct than conventional mortises and tenons. Unlike most other types of joinery, you can cut parts for loose tenons to their final length without having to take into account the extra length needed for the joint.

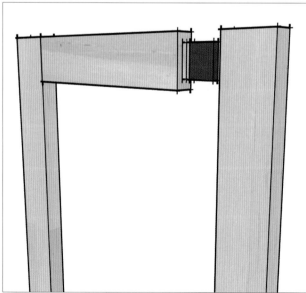

BY HAND

TOOLS NEEDED:

- Square
- Saddle square
- Marking gauge or combination square
- Drill
- Bradpoint drill bit
- Dowel jig
- Chisels
- Saws
- Small block plane

Admittedly, creating loose tenon joinery by machine is quicker and more consistent. But you most certainly can make these joints using hand tools with a little practice.

1 The layout work for loose tenon joinery is the same whether you use hand tools or machines. Assemble the joints and mark across the joint line.

2 It's customary to use the midpoint of the joint line for marking the mortise locations.

3 Extend the layout line around the end of the rail.

4 Likewise, extend the layout line around to the edge of the adjoining piece (stile).

5 The layout lines designate the center of the mortise length.

6 Use a marking gauge or combination square to scribe a line down the center to designate the midpoint of the mortise width on the stile.

TIP

When marking the centerlines, be sure to reference off the front appearance, or "good," side of the workpieces. This ensures the joints on the front of the frames are flush when assembled, regardless of minor variations in thickness. It is customary to mark the appearance side as shown here. Also, be mindful of these marks when cutting the joinery.

WORKSHOP NOTES
DOWELING JIG

You can use any method you feel comfortable with to cut the mortises in the edges of the stiles. (See the Mortise-and-tenon Joint on pages 50–61.) However, creating mortises with hand tools in the end grain of the rails presents some challenges. Using chisels, it's very likely that you could split the wood.

Instead, use a dowel jig and a portable drill equipped with a bradpoint bit to drill overlapping holes, then clean up the mortise walls with a chisel. The dowel jig assists in accurately positioning the holes while the bradpoint bit drills clean holes without tearout. And since you're using a dowel jig on the rails, you could also use it to create the stile mortises.

7 Scribe a centerline on the end of the rail.

8 A self-centering dowel jig works great for drilling into end grain. The cutting spurs on a bradpoint drill bit create a clean hole.

9 Note the lines marking the ends of the mortise. Use these as guides when positioning the dowel jig.

10 When positioning the dowel jig, sight through the drill bushing to align the outside edge with the mortise line marked on the workpiece.

11 The two holes define the ends of the mortise.

12 Drill a series of overlapping holes, repositioning the dowel jig with each hole.

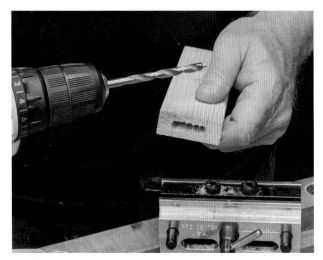

13 The series of holes removes the majority of the waste from the mortise.

14 Use a sharp chisel to clean up the remaining waste to create smooth walls in the drilled mortise.

15 After cleanup, this mortise is ready for a loose tenon.

16 After ripping long tenon stock to width and thickness to fit the mortises, round over the edges with a small block plane or sandpaper.

17 Cut the tenons to length. Make them about 1/16in (1.5mm) shorter than the combined width of the joined mortises to allow room for glue.

BY MACHINE

TOOLS NEEDED:

- Router table
- Handheld plunge router
- Straight or spiral bit
- 1/8in (3mm) radius roundover bit
- Square
- Japanese saw
- Small block plane

A handheld plunge router is an ideal tool for creating mortises. Equipped with a straight or spiral bit, it creates clean, straight mortises in almost no time.

To use a plunge router for mortising, securing the workpiece and accurately positioning it under the bit is critical. There is a wide range of commercial mortising jigs available and no shortage of shop-made jigs you can find on the internet.

WORKSHOP NOTES

SHOP-MADE ROUTER MORTISING JIG

Right: Here is a simple platform you can make for your router that helps with routing mortises. It's made from ½in (12mm) Baltic birch plywood and a 2x4 (50mm x 100mm). You'll have to build one to fit your specific router but the principle is the same. The bed features a centered slot that becomes the viewing port for centering the workpiece under the router. Two long rails guide the router left and right. A stop at each end, located between the rails, limits the travel of the router and determines the length of the mortise. The diameter of the router bit sets the width of the mortise.

Right: The 2x4 (50mm x 100mm) cleat on the underside provides a platform for securing the workpiece with a bench vise or clamps. Its position from the centerline of the viewing port is determined by the thickness of stock you'll be routing. For ¾in (20mm) thick stock, position the cleat 3/8in (10mm) back from the centerline to center mortises on the edge of the workpiece.

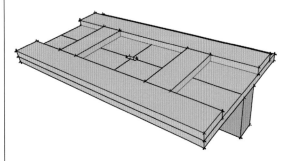

Left: To use the jig, mark on the workpiece the center point of the mortise to be routed. Place the workpiece under the base of the jig and against the cleat. Center the marked mortise location under the viewing port. Securely clamp the workpiece. Slowly lower the router bit while moving it left and right to create the mortise to full depth.

1 Mark the "show" face of each workpiece and the center point of the mortises to be routed.

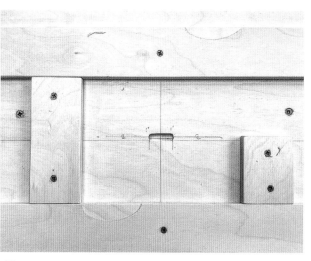

2 Center the marked mortise layout line in the mortise jig.

3 Slide the router left and right while slowly plunging the bit to the full depth of the mortise.

4 The router creates clean mortises ready for assembly.

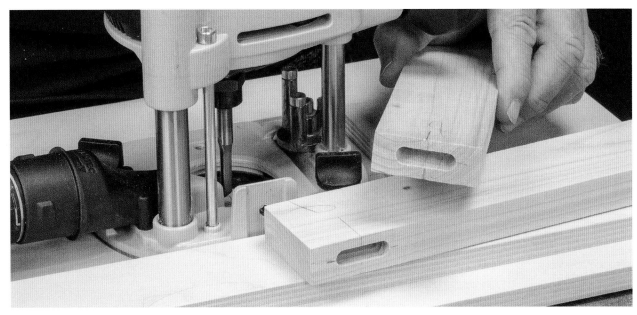

5 Repeat the process with the ends of the rails clamped securely vertically to the router jig with the mortise layout lines centered on the jig.

6 Create your own loose tenons from hardwood. Rip a strip of hardwood to width and thickness to fit the mortises. It's a good idea to make the stock just a bit narrower than the length of the tenon. This provides a little room for adjusting the workpieces during glue-up. For the thickness of the tenon stock, ensure it fits snuggly into the mortise. To assemble a strong joint, orient the grain of the tenon perpendicular to the joint line.

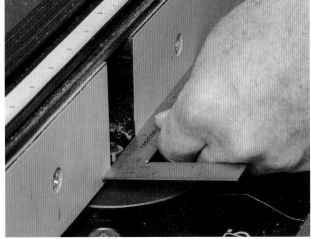

7 After ripping tenon stock to width and thickness, round over the edges at the router table using a 1/8in (3mm) radius roundover bit. Use a straightedge to align the bearing on the bit with the face of the fence.

8 Round over all the long edges of the tenon stock.

9 Cut the loose tenons to length, making them slightly shorter than the combined depth of the two joined mortises. This allows room for glue during assembly.

WORKSHOP NOTES
FESTOOL DOMINO

One power tool specifically designed for loose tenon joinery is the Festool Domino. It features a bit, much like a router bit, that oscillates left and right to create a mortise. Aligning the cursor on the tool's base with your layout line designating the center of the mortise, simply turn on the switch, then slide the body of the tool forward.

Above: While the Festool Domino might be quite the investment, it offers quick payback if you construct a lot of projects using loose tenon joinery.

Left: The Domino allows you to create mortises in a wide variety of sizes. Pressed wood loose tenons, or "dominos," in corresponding sizes make for super fast and strong joinery.

ABOUT THE AUTHOR

Randall Maxey has been woodworking for most of his life. He has contributed to other woodworking books by GMC Publications: *Outdoor Woodworking Games: 20 Fun Projects to Make* and *Woodworking Basics: The Principles and Skills of Good Joinery,* and *Sharpening: A Woodworker's Guide.*

He is a contributing editor to *Furniture & Cabinetmaking, Woodworking Crafts,* and *WOOD* magazines.

When he's not in the workshop, he can often be found outdoors with camera in hand pursuing his hobby of photography.

He resides with his wife in Florida.

ACKNOWLEDGEMENTS

Writing a book is always a time-consuming process with many challenges. Thanks to my wife, Sheryl, for her understanding and moral support when I had my head buried in my computer keyboard or in the workshop for many hours shooting photos and developing content.

Thanks to the following companies for their support:

Woodcraft
woodcraft.com

Rockler
rockler.com

Lee Valley
leevalley.com

Festool USA
festoolusa.com

Leigh
leightools.com

Woodpeckers
woodpeck.com

Infinity Tools
infinitytools.com

First published 2024 by

Guild of Master Craftsman Publications Ltd

Castle Place, 166 High Street, Lewes,

East Sussex BN7 1XU

Text © Randall A. Maxey, 2024

Copyright in the Work © GMC Publications Ltd, 2024

ISBN-13: 9781784946579

Publisher Jonathan Bailey

Production Manager Jim Bulley

Project Editor Karen Scott

Managing Art Editor Robin Shields

Designer Jonathan Bacon

Photographer Randall A. Maxey,
except; Shutterstock.com pages 17, bottom right, 41 & 131
Anthony Bailey/GMC Publications pages 15, bottom & 16 main

Colour origination by GMC Reprographics

Printed and bound in China

To place an order, contact:

GMC Publications Ltd

Castle Place, 166 High Street,

Lewes, East Sussex,

BN7 1XU United Kingdom

Tel: +44 (0)1273 488005

www.gmcbooks.com